AMERICA the BEAUTIFUL
VERMONT

By Sylvia McNair

Consultants

William Doyle, Ed.D., Professor of History and Government, Johnson State College, Montpelier; author of *The Vermont Political Tradition*

Michael Sherman, Director, Vermont Historical Society, Montpelier

Robert L. Hillerich, Ph.D., Bowling Green State University, Bowling Green, Ohio

CHILDRENS PRESS®
CHICAGO

The Apples and Crafts Fair, Woodstock

Project Editor: Joan Downing
Associate Editor: Shari Joffe
Design Director: Margrit Fiddle
Typesetting: Graphic Connections, Inc.
Engraving: Liberty Photoengraving

Library of Congress Cataloging-in-Publication Data

McNair, Sylvia.
  America the beautiful. Vermont / by Sylvia
McNair.
    p.   cm.
  Includes index.
  Summary: Introduces the geography, history,
government, economy, industry, culture, historic
sites, and famous people of Vermont.
  ISBN 0-516-00491-3
  1. Vermont—Juvenile literature.
[1. Vermont] I. Title. II. Title: Vermont.
F49.3.M37   1991   90-21117
974.3—dc20   CIP
                                            AC

Straining sap for maple syrup

TABLE OF CONTENTS

Chapter 1
THE GREEN MOUNTAIN STATE

THE GREEN MOUNTAIN STATE

Vermonters, like people everywhere, come in all sizes, shapes, and colors, all kinds of religious and political persuasions, and every variation of character. Just the same, there is a stereotypical "Vermonter" whose personality has been sculpted by the landscape and environment of a state that is not quite like any other place in the world.

Vermonters appreciate the beauty all around, and never take the splendid mountains, forests, lakes, and rivers for granted. At the same time, Vermonters know that nature, however beautiful, is not always kind. The soil of Vermont does not yield an easy living for the farmer. All Vermonters, rich or poor, have to endure bitterly cold mornings when everything is covered with ice, and getting a car started or waiting for a school bus is a painful experience.

In many ways, Vermonters are conservative. The state has limited revenues, and resources must be used carefully. Vermonters have a sense of history that makes them reluctant to change—some things. At the same time, they have been among the most imaginative and daring citizens in other directions. They have pioneered strict laws to prohibit billboards from hiding the scenery, to keep roadways free of litter, and to prevent developers from promoting uncontrolled growth.

Many generations of Vermonters have faced the challenges of poor farmland, rough climate, and isolation for the rewards of an independent lifestyle and the privilege of living in one of the world's loveliest places.

Chapter 2

THE LAND

THE LAND

Vermont's nickname, the Green Mountain State, describes exactly what the land of this state is all about. Wherever you stand in the state, you will see mountains in some direction—often in every direction. There are 420 named peaks within the tiny state. The tree-covered hills range from gentle slopes to steep mountains, with very little flat land in between.

The state's boundaries are shared with New Hampshire on the east, Massachusetts on the south, New York State on the west, and the Canadian province of Quebec on the north. Nearly half the western boundary is in Lake Champlain. Of the lake's 440 square miles (1,140 square kilometers), Vermont owns 270 square miles (699 square kilometers). The rest of the lake belongs to New York and Quebec. On the other hand, the Connecticut River, between Vermont and New Hampshire, belongs entirely to New Hampshire. Vermont is the only New England state that does not have an ocean border.

The state is small, only 158 miles (254 kilometers) from north to south and 97 miles (156 kilometers) from east to west at its widest part. With 9,614 square miles (24,900 square kilometers) of land, Vermont ranks forty-third in size among the states. It is the second-largest New England state, after Maine.

This South Woodstock sugarhouse is located in the Vermont Piedmont.

GEOGRAPHIC REGIONS

Vermont has six geographic, or physical, regions. They are the Champlain Valley, the Taconic Mountains, the Valley of Vermont, the Green Mountains, the Vermont Piedmont, and the Northeast Highlands.

The Champlain Valley, which lies between Lake Champlain and the Green Mountain range, has the flattest land, the warmest temperatures, and the best soil in the state. This combination of assets makes it the best part of the state for farming. The Champlain Valley also contains the state's largest city, Burlington, with about 38,000 residents.

South of the Champlain Valley, extending into New York and Massachusetts, is the Taconic Mountain range, which may once have been a part of the Green Mountains. Equinox Mountain at

11

3,816 feet (1,163 meters) and Dorset Peak at 3,770 feet (1,149 meters) are the Taconic's highest peaks. Marble and slate, the bedrock of these hills, have been quarried there for 150 years. Swift-running streams cut through the mountains, and scenic lakes abound.

East of the Taconics is a narrow strip, only about 5 miles (8 kilometers) wide, called the Valley of Vermont. This region, too, is famous for its fine marble quarries.

The Green Mountains make up the best-known region of the state. Running up the middle of the state from Massachusetts to Canada, they are often called the backbone of Vermont—a backbone that varies from 20 to 36 miles (32 to 58 kilometers) in width. Millions of years ago, the Green Mountains were nearly as high as any that exist in the world today. Then huge glaciers moved down from the north, wearing down the mountains and scattering rocks everywhere.

The state's highest point—4,393-foot (1,339-meter) Mount Mansfield—stands in this range. Killington Mountain, Mount Ellen, and Camels Hump are the range's next highest peaks. Talc, granite, marble, and asbestos are mined or quarried in the Green Mountains, but they are most prized for their scenery and recreational areas. Skiing, hiking, biking, and mountain climbing are popular activities in the Green Mountains.

East of the Green Mountains is the Vermont Piedmont, the state's largest physical region. Narrow river valleys cut through the hills, and clear, cold lakes are scattered about. Deposits of fine-quality granite are an important asset of the region. Broad lowlands, with good soil for dairy farming, lie along the Connecticut River.

The sixth region of the state is the Northeast Highlands, popularly called the Northeast Kingdom. This region is part of

Lake St. Catherine (left), near Poultney, is one of nearly 430 lakes and ponds in Vermont. Moss Glen Falls (right) tumbles over the rocks in Green Mountain National Forest.

New Hampshire's White Mountain range. The Northeast Highland's highest peaks are Gore Mountain, at 3,330 feet (1,015 meters), and Burke Mountain, at 3,267 feet (996 meters). Swift streams run through the mountains on their way to the Connecticut River. Much of the region's acreage is still forested wilderness, owned by large lumber companies.

LAKES AND RIVERS

Vermont is abundantly blessed with fresh water. It tumbles off the hills and mountains in picturesque waterfalls, gushes from springs, gurgles over rocky brooks, runs through rivers, and gathers in mirrorlike lakes.

Most Vermont towns and villages were settled along rivers. They served as transportation routes for American Indians and

Sunset, Lake Champlain

early settlers; later they were a source of waterpower to run small mills and factories. Frozen solid during long, severe winters, the rivers become skating rinks and even pathways for sleigh racing. Every spring, nature puts on a show along the rivers. Warmer temperatures break up the ice into huge chunks that come rushing downstream, sometimes causing ice jams and spring floods.

Otter Creek, flowing 100 miles (161 kilometers) north into Lake Champlain, is Vermont's longest river. Three large rivers in northwestern Vermont are the Missisquoi, Lamoille, and Winooski, all of which also flow into Lake Champlain. The Batten Kill and Walloomsac rivers in the southwest run into other rivers in New York. In the east, the Passumpsic, White, Black, and West rivers empty into the Connecticut River.

There are nearly 430 lakes and ponds in the state. They are a major source of recreation and scenic beauty. Summer homes and camps line the shores of most of them.

Largest of the lakes is Lake Champlain. Like the Green Mountains, Lake Champlain was created eons ago by glacial action. Isle La Motte, one of the lake's islands, claims to have the oldest offshore coral reef in the world. In the seventeenth century, French explorers and trappers used the lake as a route into the region south of Canada. Today, boaters, fishers, campers, and other vacationers enjoy the lake's beauty in summer.

Two thirds of Lake Memphremagog, Vermont's second-largest lake, lies in Quebec. The largest lake totally within the state is Lake Bomoseen, west of Rutland. Many other lakes, such as Seymour, Crystal, and Maidstone lakes and Lake Salem, are in the northeastern part of the state.

PLANTS AND ANIMALS

Forests cover about four-fifths of Vermont's acreage. Green Mountain National Forest, in two sections in the middle of the state, contains 630,000 acres (254,955 hectares). The state tree is the sugar maple, valuable for the production of maple syrup as well as for its fine hard wood. Other plentiful deciduous, or hardwood, trees are birch, beech, ash, poplar, basswood, and oak. Common softwoods, also called evergreens or conifers, are spruce, pine, hemlock, and cedar.

Vermont's hillsides and forests are famous for the brilliance of their fall foliage. Maple trees produce vivid reds and oranges, birches turn bright yellow, tamaracks become golden, and oaks a deep maroon. These shining colors are splashed against the darker shades of giant evergreens.

Native plants include many kinds of ferns, grasses, and sedges. Pussy willows and more than twelve hundred kinds of wildflowers, such as anemones, arbutus, asters, bloodroots,

Marsh marigolds (left), members of the buttercup family, and asters (right) are among the hundreds of kinds of wildflowers that are native to the state.

buttercups, daisies, Dutchman's-breeches, gentians, goldenrod, jack-in-the-pulpits, violets, and red clover, the state flower, add color to Vermont's countryside.

Vermont's forests provide good homes for white-tailed deer, muskrats, skunks, raccoons, foxes, minks, and some bears and bobcats. Smaller native animals are rabbits, squirrels, woodchucks, and hedgehogs. Birds finding homes in the state's trees include ravens, saw-whet owls, cardinals, nuthatches, and hermit thrushes, the state bird. Vermont's rivers and lakes provide nesting areas for loons and geese and spawning grounds for brook or lake trout, catfish, perch, salmon, and walleyes.

CLIMATE

Winters are long, cold, and snowy in Vermont, often lasting from early November until mid-April. Average snowfall ranges

Small children struggle through deep snowdrifts during a typical Vermont winter.

from 60 to 80 inches (152 to 203 centimeters) in the lowlands to 80 to 120 inches (203 to 305 centimeters) in the mountains of northern Vermont. Roads and highways are bordered with high snowbanks and the entire landscape is covered with a white blanket for months. A record low temperature of minus 50 degrees Fahrenheit (minus 46 degrees Celsius) was recorded at Bloomfield on December 30, 1933. The average January temperature for the state is 17 degrees Fahrenheit (minus 8 degrees Celsius).

The short summers consist of mild days—rarely hot—and cool evenings. The average July temperature is 68 degrees Fahrenheit (20 degrees Celsius). On July 4, 1911, the state's record high was set in Vernon when the mercury soared to 105 degrees Fahrenheit (41 degrees Celsius). Heavy rains generally fall in early summer. Precipitation—rain and melted snow—averages 39 inches (99 centimeters) a year. The growing season is short, barely one hundred days in the northern part of the state.

Chapter 3
THE PEOPLE

THE PEOPLE

There is a certain mystique about Vermont and Vermonters. Anyone who has ever lived there believes in the uniqueness of the Vermont character, and visitors to the state soon believe it too. One writer has described a typical Vermonter as one who does not conform to any type. "Each of them is an original," she wrote.

POPULATION AND POPULATION DISTRIBUTION

When Vermont became a state, in 1791, fewer than 90,000 people lived there. During the first fifty years of statehood, the population more than tripled, to nearly 300,000. During the next hundred years, however, growth was slow, with only another 67,000 residents being added. Few other states grew as slowly. Thin, rocky soil made it difficult to make a good living from farming. In addition, factory work was scarce because Vermont did not keep pace with the Industrial Revolution as did Massachusetts and Connecticut, its New England neighbors to the south.

Between 1945 and 1990, however, many new residents moved to Vermont. In those forty-five years, the population increase was about three times as great as it had been in the previous century. According to the 1980 census, the population was 511,456—more than a half-million people.

Vermont, however, remains a lightly populated state and ranks forty-eighth among the states. Only Alaska and Wyoming have fewer residents. In fact, more than twenty cities in the United States have more residents than the entire state of Vermont!

Two-thirds of the people in Vermont are classified as rural by the United States Bureau of the Census. This means that they live in the country or in villages with fewer than 2,500 people. Vermont's proportion of rural residents is the highest of any state.

Burlington, the state's largest city, has only 37,712 people. Only two other cities—Rutland and South Burlington—have more than 10,000 residents. The Burlington metropolitan area is home to 115,308 Vermonters—almost one-fourth of the state's population.

Vermont's population density is 53 persons per square mile (20 persons per square kilometer), compared with 67 persons per square mile (26 persons per square kilometer) for the United States. The largest populated areas are located along the Connecticut River, Lake Champlain, and the Vermont Valley.

WHO ARE THE VERMONTERS?

Between 1760 and 1840, most of the pioneers who ventured into Vermont were Yankees—people from southern New England—and New Yorkers. Young people from Connecticut and Massachusetts traveled up the river valleys to start new homesteads on the rocky hillsides of Vermont.

In the 1840s, Irish immigrants began to trickle into the state, finding work building railroads. Following them came Scots, Italians, Spaniards, Swedes, and Welsh, attracted by jobs in the granite, marble, and slate quarries. Small pockets of Poles and Portuguese settled in cities such as Springfield and Brattleboro. A few Finns came to farm in the southern part of the state.

Over the years, the largest number of immigrants have been French-speaking Canadians from Quebec. As recently as 1970,

Two-thirds of Vermonters live in the country or in villages with fewer than 2,500 people.

nearly 9 percent of the state's population were either born in Quebec or had at least one parent from there. French remains their mother tongue. In 1980, first- and second-generation Italians made up about 4 percent of the population.

About two thousand descendants of the region's earliest residents—the Abenaki nation—live in the northwestern corner of the state. For much of the state's history, they were almost an underground community, quiet and unassertive. But in the 1970s, the Abenakis, along with many other ethnic groups, experienced a renewed sense of pride in their ancestry and traditions. Through the efforts of an elected tribal council, self-help ventures such as adult-education programs, day-care centers for children, and low-cost housing projects have been established.

Many of the nearly two hundred thousand newcomers in the past four decades have moved in from other states, but other countries have also contributed to the state's growth. Cambodia, Vietnam, Laos, Ethiopia, the Soviet Union, Poland, Korea, China, Japan, India, and Guatemala are among the former homes of some of Vermont's more recent immigrants.

Today, Vermont's foreign-born population is only 4 percent. The nonwhite population is less than 1 percent and is composed of about two thousand blacks, two thousand Native Americans, and thirteen hundred Asians.

RELIGION

The Roman Catholic church has more members than any other church in the state. Major Protestant denominations include United Methodists, United Church of Christ (formerly called Congregationalists), American Baptists, and Episcopalians. There is a small Jewish population, and some of the recent Asian immigrants have brought Buddhism to Vermont.

Two religious sects have their seeds in Vermont's rocky soil. The Holy Rollers originated in Hardwick, Vermont. The Church of Jesus Christ of Latter-day Saints (Mormons) was founded in 1830 in New York by Joseph Smith of Sharon. In 1844, Brigham Young of Whitingham became the church's leader.

POLITICS

Until 1958, Vermont could be counted on more than any other state to vote the Republican party ticket—for president, governor, and members of Congress. In the 1936 presidential election, only Vermont and Maine failed to produce a majority vote for the Democratic incumbent, President Franklin D. Roosevelt.

One-party rule in Vermont started to fade away in the 1950s

and 1960s. William H. Meyer was elected to the United States House of Representatives in 1958, the first Democrat from the state in more than a hundred years. Four years later another Democrat, Philip H. Hoff, broke a similar record by winning the governor's chair. And in 1974, Patrick Leahy became the first Democratic United States senator from Vermont since the founding of the Republican party in 1854.

Since those breakthroughs, competition between the two parties has been lively. Between 1962 and 1990, two Democrats, Thomas P. Salmon and Madeleine Kunin, reached the governorship.

Another political change is the increase in the influence of women. Republican Consuelo Northup Bailey became the nation's first female lieutenant governor in 1955. In 1984, Democrat Madeleine May Kunin became the first woman elected to the office of governor of Vermont. With Kunin's election, the Democrats also won a majority of the seats in both houses of the state legislature. In 1989, Vermont had a greater percentage of women legislators than any other state legislature in the nation — about 33 percent.

According to most observers, these changes show a growth of independence in politics — a philosophy of voting for individuals rather than for a party.

In Burlington, Bernard Sanders became the only Socialist mayor in the nation in 1981 and was reelected in 1983, 1985, and 1986. In 1990, Sanders was elected Vermont's United States representative, becoming the first Socialist elected to the U. S. House in sixty years. At the same time, Vermonters elected Republican Richard Snelling governor and Democrat Howard Dean lieutenant governor. During the 1980s, however, Vermonters cast their presidential ballots for Republicans Ronald Reagan in 1980 and 1984 and George Bush in 1988.

Chapter 4
BEFORE STATEHOOD

BEFORE STATEHOOD

INDIANS IN VERMONT

Before European explorers and settlers entered what is now known as Vermont, American Indians used the region as a hunting ground. The Abenaki, Mahican, and Penacook—all Algonquian-speaking tribes—claimed this territory until the 1500s. At that time, powerful tribes from the Iroquois Nation, based in present-day New York, began to occupy the area. When the French arrived in the early 1600s, they formed an alliance with the Algonquians.

Many place names in Vermont, such as the Winooski, Passumpsic, and Nulhegan rivers and the Ascutney and Pico mountains, are derived from American Indian words. Remains of temporary Indian settlements have been found at Orwell, Newbury, Swanton, and Vernon. Indian petroglyphs—pictures carved in rocks—can be seen along the Connecticut River at Bellows Falls.

EUROPEAN EXPLORERS AND SETTLERS

French explorer Samuel de Champlain came to North America in the early 1600s. After founding settlements at Quebec and Montreal, in what is now Canada, he and a party of Algonquians traveled south on the Richelieu River into a large lake.

The first historical record of Europeans in Vermont is Champlain's journal entry about finding a lake filled with

Settlement of Vermont didn't begin until the mid-1700s.

beautiful islands on July 4, 1609. Champlain claimed the Vermont region for France. The lake was later named after him.

The French built a few military posts in the region, but they did not establish any permanent settlements. Fort St. Anne, built on Isle La Motte in 1666, is believed to have been the first of these military outposts. The French were interested in this region mainly for the fur trade with the Algonquians.

Meanwhile, English colonists were settling in the neighboring New England colonies of New Hampshire and Massachusetts. English and Dutch settlers were building homes in the New York colony. But the Vermont area remained a wilderness.

In 1724, more than a hundred years after Champlain's voyage, the English built Fort Dummer in the far southeastern corner of present-day Vermont to protect settlers in Massachusetts from raids by the French and Indians. The fort became the first permanent white settlement in Vermont. In that same year, a group of Dutch settled in the far southwestern corner near present-day Pownal. In 1731, to protect their interests in the area, the French built a fort at present-day Crown Point on the New York side of Lake Champlain.

During those early years, the Vermont region's importance lay in its water routes for the fur trade. The Connecticut River in the east opened the way to eastern and southern New England. Lake Champlain in the northwest served as an entryway to the New York colony.

THE NEW HAMPSHIRE GRANTS

Due to the work of Benning Wentworth, the royal governor of New Hampshire, the settlement of Vermont finally started. Wentworth had some pressing debts to pay off, and he decided to raise money by selling vacant land west of the Connecticut River. Although Wentworth thought that New Hampshire's western boundary should extend to New York, just as the Massachusetts boundary did, he probably was not at all sure that he had any authority to make the sale. Like many another settler in primitive societies all over the world, however, he decided to act as if he did have the authority.

In 1750, Wentworth granted a township, named Bennington after his own first name, to some of his friends and relatives. Between 1750 and 1764, he granted charters for 138 towns, covering about 3 million acres (1.2 million hectares) of land. Wentworth sold the land at one-half cent per acre (one-half cent per 0.4 hectares). The area became known as the New Hampshire Grants. The deals made Wentworth rich; he paid his debts and built a mansion in Portsmouth, New Hampshire.

During these same years, Governor George Clinton of New York thought that the territory east of his colony, extending to the

Connecticut River, was part of New York. He also began making claims in Vermont.

Between 1754 and 1763, during the controversy over land in Vermont, the French and Indian War was being waged. Much fighting took place in the Lake Champlain region since the area was claimed by both the French and the English. The English, with their Iroquois allies, pushed the French and the Algonquians from the area. In 1763, the Treaty of Paris granted England control of the Vermont territory, as well as all French lands in Canada and east of the Mississippi River.

Once the war was over, Clinton approached King George III of England, who backed his claim in 1764. Governor Clinton informed the thousand or so settlers in the "Grants" that they would have to pay New York for their land. In 1767, the grant holders sent a petition to the king pleading their cause. The king decreed that Clinton was not to bother the New Hampshire Grants' settlers and was not to issue further grants.

This decree did not end the controversy, however. In 1769 and 1770, New York issued titles to 600,000 acres (242,814 hectares) in the Grants, sent surveyors to plot the land, and filed ejection suits against the settlers who were already there.

THE GREEN MOUNTAIN BOYS

A group of "Hampshiremen," settlers in Vermont who held land grants from New Hampshire, met to decide what to do about the threats from the New York colonial government. They called themselves the Bennington Nine. Ethan Allen, who later made a name as a hero of the Revolutionary War, was elected to be their spokesperson in fighting New York's claims. Allen first tried to settle matters in court. When that didn't work, he assembled a

Ethan Allen (center) and the Green Mountain Boys drove out New York families who tried to settle on land acquired under the New Hampshire Grants.

group of settlers who were determined to protect their land by force, if necessary.

In 1770, about two hundred men met with Ethan Allen at the Catamount Tavern, in Bennington. They organized into a regiment and gave themselves a name, the Green Mountain Boys. Their symbol was the catamount, the powerful and stealthy panther that was common in the forests of New England at the time. Ann Story gained fame as a spy for Allen's military operation.

For the next few years, the Green Mountain Boys acted as protectors of the lands acquired under the New Hampshire Grants, driving out families who tried to settle land obtained through New York titles. New Yorkers considered Allen's men outlaws. They called them the Bennington Mob.

THE REVOLUTIONARY WAR

In April 1775, events outside of Vermont captured the attention of the Green Mountain Boys. British soldiers entered into armed conflict with colonials called Minutemen, at Lexington and Concord, Massachusetts—the first battle of the Revolutionary War.

The Green Mountain Boys went into action. In May 1775, they captured Fort Ticonderoga, a British military post near the southern tip of Lake Champlain, in New York. Ethan Allen and his men surprised the British sentry at dawn, and the fort was seized without the firing of a single shot. The British commander asked by whose authority Allen was demanding surrender, and was told it was "in the name of the great Jehovah and the Continental Congress!" Soon the Green Mountain Boys had captured another British outpost at Crown Point, north of Ticonderoga. Then they seized a British ship at St. John, on the Richelieu River in Canada. This gave the Americans complete control of the Champlain Valley.

It seems inconsistent that the Green Mountain Boys would choose so quickly to fight the British. The New Yorkers were the enemy they had banded together to fight, and British agents had supported their claims against New York. Ethan Allen explained their position by claiming that the raid on Fort Ticonderoga was the result of a "sincere passion for liberty."

Whether or not Allen's motives were sincere, it is a fact that the four Allen brothers and their cousin, Remember Baker, were interested in doing whatever they could to ensure their own landed interests. They were speculators and, heroes or not, they were also clever opportunists. They probably reasoned that capturing Fort Ticonderoga could strengthen their own—and

Vermont's—claims to land on the western side of Lake Champlain.

The Green Mountain Boys persuaded the American colonists to take them into the Continental army. Seth Warner was chosen to command the regiment. Plans were laid to carry the fighting into Canada. In 1775, during an attack on the city of Montreal, Ethan Allen was captured by the British and spent more than two years as a prisoner of war.

The only Revolutionary War battle fought on Vermont soil took place in July 1777, in the village of Hubbardton. Unfortunately, the British won that battle against the Green Mountain Boys, who were led by Seth Warner.

On August 16, 1777, the Green Mountain Boys—with the help of some troops from Massachusetts—won a great victory in the Battle of Bennington. This battle was important because it led, soon after, to a resounding defeat for the British at Saratoga, a turning point of the war. The fighting, however, did not take place on Vermont soil. The clash actually occurred on the other side of the New York line, in East Hoosick. But since it was planned in Vermont and fought by Vermonters, the Battle of Bennington holds a special spot in the history of the state.

Although the British fought no more battles in Vermont, they sent their Indian allies to raid and destroy several settlements. A blockhouse at Shelburne was attacked in 1778, and Royalton was burned to the ground in 1780.

THE INDEPENDENT STATE OF VERMONT

While some Vermonters were fighting with the colonies for freedom from Britain, others were busy at home making decisions about their political future. Several conventions were held. The participants passed resolutions to pave the way for separating the "Grants" from both New Hampshire and New York.

On January 14, 1777, at a convention in Westminster, representatives of the people of the New Hampshire Grants adopted their own declaration of independence from England and New York, establishing a state called New Connecticut. Five months later, in Windsor, another convention reaffirmed the declaration but changed its name to Vermont, from the French words *vert mont*, meaning "green mountain." A constitution was adopted in July, also at Windsor. Ira Allen wrote its preamble.

The constitution of the new state was as remarkable a work as the more famous Declaration of Independence that had been written in Philadelphia in July 1776. Vermont's basic Bill of Rights has survived intact in the present state constitution.

One of the provisions in the constitution was the banning of slaveholding within Vermont's borders. With this action, Vermont became the first political body in the United States to abolish slavery. Vermont also became the first political body to grant every man, whether or not he owned property, the right to vote. The constitution gave Vermont's government the power to coin money, establish a post office, and conduct foreign policy.

The founding of an independent state did not put to rest the controversies over who had jurisdiction over Vermont's lands. Some Vermonters were Tories, or loyalists, who still hoped for a separate peace with Britain. Ethan Allen's brother Ira was responsible for a scheme that appropriated the land claimed by some of these loyalists. The land was then sold to pay the troops defending Bennington. Many Vermont loyalists migrated to Nova Scotia, in Canada.

At the same time, the Allen brothers, who held large pieces of property in the northern Champlain Valley, were playing the various sides—New York, the Continental Congress, and even Britain—against one another. They continued to confer with British agents in Quebec to protect themselves in case the colonies lost the war.

In 1778, Vermonters elected Thomas Chittenden their first governor. During the next year, Vermont confronted the Continental Congress with three actions. It charged that the Congress was endangering Vermont's liberties. It declared itself free and independent of any authority of the Congress. Finally, it declared itself free to enter into a separate treaty of peace with Britain.

Congress, busy in Philadelphia with the affairs of the thirteen colonies, ignored the independent state of Vermont. New York, New Hampshire, and Massachusetts all felt they had rights to some of the Vermont land. Vermont had no voice in the disputes taking place in the Congress.

The borders of the new state were not yet clear because of conflicting land claims. Thirty-five towns on the east side of the Connecticut River, in New Hampshire, were annexed to Vermont. At the same time, Vermont annexed fourteen New York towns, including Saratoga and Lake George. No one was sure about the exact location of the boundary between Vermont and Quebec.

Because of these controversies, members of Congress wanted to invade Vermont. General George Washington advised against this. He wrote a letter warning that the invasion was likely to fail because of the mountainous terrain and the fact that Vermonters "for the most part are a hardy race, composed of that kind of people who are best calculated for soldiers." Washington also advised Chittenden to drop the claims to the thirty-five New Hampshire towns and the fourteen New York towns.

Ethan Allen's home in Burlington was built in 1787.

In 1783, after the Revolutionary War, the Treaty of Paris established the southern boundary of Canada at the 45th parallel, and the idea that Vermont might become a part of Canada died. Peace between Vermont and New York was achieved in 1790 when Vermont paid $30,000 for disputed land within its borders. The way was now ready for statehood, and on March 4, 1791, Vermont became the fourteenth state in the Union.

Vermont had remained an independent state for only fourteen years. During that time, Vermonters established a heritage of independent thinking and action that has been a hallmark of the state ever since. Vermonters today like to point out that their land was never an English colony and that the original settlers formed their own state.

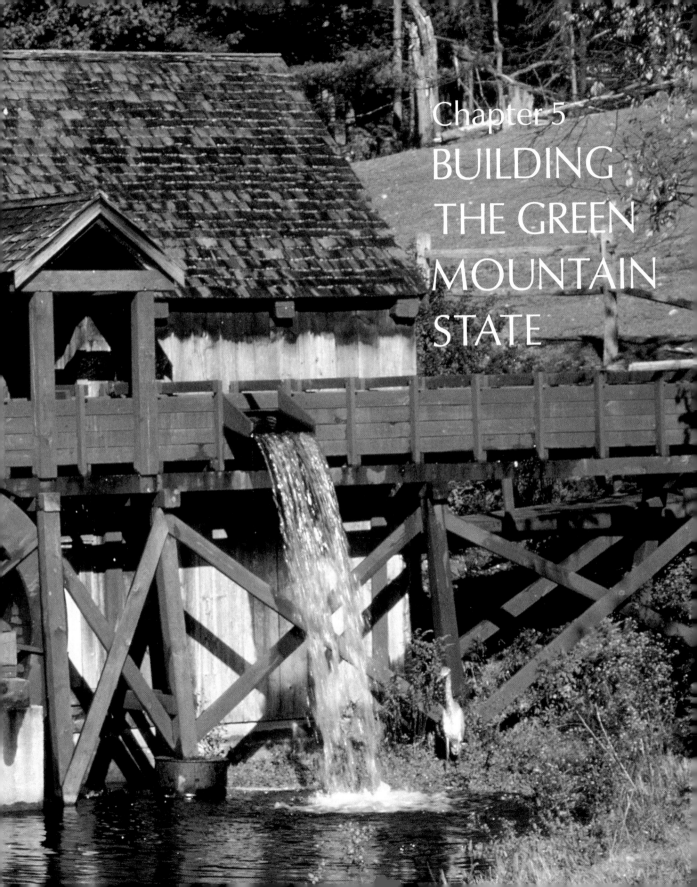

Chapter 5

BUILDING THE GREEN MOUNTAIN STATE

BUILDING THE GREEN MOUNTAIN STATE

EARLY GROWTH AND PROSPERITY

Vermont was part of America's first frontier. The first Vermonters were sons and daughters of settlers from the New England and New York colonies. They were looking for land of their own in which to put down roots. During its fourteen years as an independent state, Vermont's population more than tripled to 85,425 as new settlers poured in. In the first twenty years of statehood, the population more than doubled, to 217,895 people. According to census records, two-thirds of the 1800 population were under twenty-six years old.

These young people who lived in Vermont's hills and river valleys cleared the forests, built homes, established farms, and started businesses. Education was important to the early Vermonters. In 1791, the University of Vermont was chartered, followed nine years later by Middlebury College. Also in 1791, the state's first library opened in Brookfield.

Some of Vermont's first industries relied on its water and timber resources. Gristmills, paper mills, and sawmills were built along fast-moving streams. Logs were floated down the Connecticut River to paper plants and wood-turning factories and up Lake Champlain to Canadian cities on the St. Lawrence River. By 1805, Brattleboro was developing as a printing center. Brandon, Tinmouth, and Vergennes became the state's iron-mining centers.

Justin Morgan was the first of Vermont's special breed called the Morgan horse.

To plow their hilly farms, Vermonters began to rely on the Morgan horse, the first special breed of horse developed in the United States. In 1791, Justin Morgan bought a fast, gentle, two-year-old horse for riding. Soon after, he fell ill and rented the horse to farmers for clearing land and plowing. First known as Justin Morgan's horse, and after his master's death as Justin Morgan, the horse developed tremendous leg and chest muscles from this hard work. During his thirty-two years, the horse sired many descendants, called Morgan horses. They were prized by Vermont farmers for their strength, speed, beauty, and gentleness.

Improvements in transportation were made. Samuel Morey operated a steamboat on the Connecticut River in 1793. In 1802, the first canal built in the United States opened at Bellows Falls on the Connecticut River. In 1808, the steamboat *Vermont* began moving people and goods on Lake Champlain. The following

Steamboats began operating on Lake Champlain in 1808.

year, steamboat service linked Vermont to New York State and
St. John, Canada. Much of Vermont's early prosperity came from
this trade with Canada.

In the early 1800s, England and France were at war with each
other. The United States tried to stay neutral and carry on trade
with both countries. Both France and England, however, seized
American ships that were trading with the other country.

To stop these actions, President Thomas Jefferson signed the
Embargo Act in 1807, ordering all trade with foreign countries to
stop. In 1809, a new law stated that only trade with England and
France and lands under their control was illegal. These laws were
unpopular in Vermont because of the trade with Canada. Many
Vermonters, especially in the Lake Champlain area, ignored the
laws and smuggled food products and lumber into Canada, which
was under British control. Vermont's economy continued to grow
during these years, however. Smugglers made huge profits, and

Spanish merino sheep were imported to Vermont in 1811.

the state's factories expanded to produce manufactured goods that had previously been imported from Europe.

One of these goods was wool, imported in large amounts from England before 1807. To fill the country's need for wool, William Jarvis imported 350 Spanish merino sheep to his farm in Weathersfield Bow. They produced thick, long white wool and were especially suited to Vermont's climate and terrain. Thousands more merino sheep were imported and bred in the following years. With the growth of sheep raising, tanneries to process the skins and carding mills to comb the wool into spinning yarn were built in Vermont.

At first, yarn spinning and weaving were done in homes. The homespun cloth was then taken to fulling, or cleansing, mills where it was washed, shrunk, and smoothed into more attractive cloth. Later, all these processes—carding, spinning, weaving, and fulling—were done in textile factories.

WAR OF 1812

When England continued to harass American ships, the United States declared war in 1812. The war was very unpopular among Vermonters. Citizens in the northern part of the state feared an invasion from Canada, and some of the towns there were abandoned. The smuggling of food products to Canada persisted, and the governor general of Canada reported in 1814 that "two-thirds of the army in Canada are . . . eating beef provided by American contractors, drawn principally from the states of Vermont and New York."

While smugglers made illegal profits, sheep farmers and owners of woolen mills made large profits from legal trade. Since wool was needed for the American army's blankets and uniforms, wool prices climbed.

Vermonters also helped in the war effort. During the winter of 1813-14, Lieutenant Thomas Macdonough sailed his fleet from Lake Champlain up Otter Creek to Vergennes. At the shipyards there, shipbuilders using Vermont timber turned out finished ships at the rate of one every forty days. By summer, Macdonough had a new fleet. In October, at the Battle of Plattsburgh in New York, these ships, staffed with many Vermont farmers, helped defeat the British. The entire Lake Champlain area came firmly under American control. Many Vermonters also helped the American cause during the land battle at Plattsburgh.

ECONOMIC CHANGES

With the end of the war, late in 1814, trade with England resumed. Low-priced cotton and woolen cloth, as well as other manufactured goods from England, flooded Vermont's shops. The

During the War of 1812, a fleet of ships built with Vermont timber and staffed with many Vermont farmers helped defeat the British at the Battle of Plattsburgh.

price of Vermont wool went down. In 1810, Vermont's manufactured goods were worth more than $5 million. By 1820, their value had fallen to less than $1 million. During those years, thousands of Vermonters left the state. They could no longer endure the economic hard times, which were made worse by floods, grasshopper plagues, and a cold spell that lasted from 1812 to 1818.

Conditions improved for farmers in the Champlain Valley when the Champlain-Hudson Canal opened in 1823, connecting Lake Champlain to New York's Hudson River. Vermont's farm goods and wool were shipped all the way to New York City. When the Erie Canal opened in 1825, linking the Hudson River to Lake Erie, Vermont's trading network reached to the Great Lakes. The canals, however, made it easier for Vermonters to leave the state.

Members of the Vermont Dairymen's Association bringing milk to a local cheese factory

Through the 1830s, sheep raising remained the major source of farm income. By the late 1830s, there were eighty textile factories, plus a few knitting mills, in the state. For its size, Vermont raised more sheep and made more wool than any other state. During the late 1840s, sheep raising was on the downturn. The price of wool fell because sheep ranchers in the West, with larger flocks on open range, could sell the wool at lower prices. Vermont's farmers could no longer afford to raise sheep.

By the 1840s, Vermonters realized they had used up much of their natural resources. The Champlain Valley's forests were depleted, fur-bearing animals had been overhunted, and there were few fish left in the streams. Overgrazing by sheep and annual plantings of the same crops had robbed Vermont's land of good topsoil. Many farmers left the state in search of rich western farmland.

Those who stayed turned to dairy farming—the mainstay of Vermont's agriculture today. The nation's first statewide dairy

In the mid-1850s, Vermont's small hotels and resorts became popular destinations for "summer people," who came to breathe the mountain air and "take the waters."

association was formed in Vermont in 1869. At about that time, the first silos built in the United States began to appear on Vermont's farms. Railroads carried milk, cheese, and butter from Vermont to New York City and to cities in Massachusetts.

Vermont's first railroad, completed in 1848, ran between Bethel and White River Junction on its way south to Boston. The next year, tracks were built to Burlington. Within the next few years, railroads carried Vermont's products to Albany and Troy, New York; Portland, Maine; and Montreal, Quebec. The railroads also brought in manufactured goods at prices lower than Vermont manufacturers could compete with.

Once again, improved transportation made it easier for Vermonters to leave. By 1850, more than 145,000 had been lured to better land or jobs in other parts of the country. Between 1820 and 1850, more than 1,000 young women found work in Massachusetts textile factories.

While many Vermonters left the state, large numbers of visitors from the South, as well as from neighboring states, came to "summer" in Vermont. "Summer people" journeyed north to breathe the cool, pure, mountain air and to "take the waters." In the nineteenth century, it was popular to drink and bathe in certain spring waters, in the belief that they had medicinal benefits and could even cure some diseases.

Small hotels and resorts were established in Middletown Springs, Sheldon Springs, Plainfield, Guilford, and Brunswick. President Martin Van Buren, Henry Wadsworth Longfellow, and Harriet Beecher Stowe visited Whetston Brook, in Brattleboro. Some of the visitors, including Robert Todd Lincoln, stayed and built large summer homes in the mountains. During the Civil War, southerners discontinued their summer visits.

RELIGIOUS AND SOCIAL REFORM MOVEMENTS

During the same years that Vermonters were experiencing economic changes, many of the state's citizens became involved in the various reform movements that were sweeping the nation. The established churches of Massachusetts and Connecticut had not had much influence in Vermont during its formative years. Many clergymen in southern New England saw Vermont as a stronghold of atheism, drunkenness, and general sin. After all, Ethan Allen, the principal founding father of Vermont, had written and published a book that attacked traditional religion. Presbyterians, Baptists, Methodists, and Congregationalists sent missionaries into Vermont to conduct religious revivals in nearly every town during the first thirty years of the nineteenth century.

In 1838, John Humphrey Noyes, a Brattleboro native, founded a Utopian community to practice a doctrine known as Perfectionism. Perfectionists shared all their property and their

From the mid-1800s to the early 1900s, most Vermont students in grades one through eight were taught in one-room schoolhouses.

wives. Vermonters did not approve of this behavior and forced the Perfectionists to leave Vermont. The group went to New York and founded the Oneida Community, which became successful through the manufacture of silverware. The religious sect died out eventually, but Oneida silver survives today.

Another sect, known as the Millerites, flourished for a short time in the state. A man named William Miller prophesied that the world would end on March 21, 1843 or 1844. He persuaded his followers that only the righteous would be saved; the rest would perish in fire. After his prophecy failed to come true, the sect gradually disappeared.

Educational reformers were also active in Vermont. Emma Hart Willard began her pioneering work in higher education for women. In 1814, she established a women's academic boarding school in Middlebury. Improving teaching methods was important to Samuel Read Hall. In 1823, in Concord Corner, he founded the first school in the United States for the training of teachers. Hall is also credited with writing the first book about teaching and with originating the use of blackboards in schoolrooms. In 1845, the General Assembly passed a school-reform act that called for improvements in education under the supervision of a state superintendent.

Three social issues—prohibition, woman suffrage, and abolition—were hotly debated throughout the country in the mid-1800s. Prohibition advocates gained a great deal of influence. In 1852, Vermont became the second state—after Maine—to pass a law prohibiting liquor entirely. The law was not effective, however, and later the state gave individual towns the right to vote on abolishing liquor within town boundaries. Even "dry" towns often had places where alcoholic drinks were available.

The causes of prohibition and woman suffrage were closely intertwined in the nineteenth century because women were the victims of men's drunkenness. Money that should have fed the family often was spent in saloons, and wife beating was a frequent result of excessive drinking. Clarina Howard Nichols, Emma Hart Willard, and other Vermonters actively worked to improve the status of women. Efforts were made to grant women political, legal, and property rights.

Of all the social movements, the abolition of slavery had the strongest following in Vermont. Slavery had been illegal in Vermont since the days of the state's independence. Both the holding and the transporting of slaves within the state were expressly forbidden. Moreover, the farmers and the owners of small businesses in the state had little sympathy for the economic problems of the slaveholding plantation owners of the South. Many Vermont homes served as stations for the Underground Railroad—the route slaves took on their way to freedom in Canada.

Among the many reformers who were active in Vermont during the 1800s were Emma Hart Willard (left), who pioneered higher education for women, and William Lloyd Garrison (right), the nation's most prominent abolitionist.

William Lloyd Garrison, the nation's most prominent abolitionist, began his antislavery campaign in 1828 by publishing a newspaper, *The Journal of the Times,* in Bennington. When he left the state, other Vermont newspapers carried on the cause of abolition.

In 1837, the Vermont legislature sent resolutions to the United States Senate protesting the annexation of Texas as a slave state. When the Mexican War broke out in 1845 over land west of Texas, Vermont did nothing to help the United States. Vermonters felt that the new lands, if acquired, would become slave states.

Support for the antislavery cause became so strong that in the presidential election of 1860, more than three-fourths of the state's popular vote went to Abraham Lincoln. Fewer than one in five Vermonters cast a ballot for his opponent, a native Vermonter named Stephen Douglas.

The Confederate soldiers shown here in the office of a Montreal jail were among the more than twenty who robbed three St. Albans' banks in 1864.

THE CIVIL WAR

Vermonters enthusiastically gathered behind President Lincoln to support the Union cause when the Civil War broke out in 1861. The state legislature voted an appropriation of $1 million to raise and pay for troops. Altogether, Vermont's citizens, towns, and villages contributed $9,323,407 to the war effort. Some thirty-five thousand men went into service—more than one out of every ten Vermonters. About one thousand Morgan horses were used as cavalry mounts by the First Vermont Regiment. Vermont's troops took part in all the major battles in Virginia, Maryland, and Pennsylvania. More than five thousand Vermonters died in service.

In August 1864, the northernmost incident of the war took place in St. Albans. A group of more than twenty Confederate soldiers sneaked into town and held up three local banks, saying they were taking possession of the town for the Confederacy. With over $200,000, they made a dash for the nearby Canadian border. Most of the soldiers were caught by the Canadian government. For a while, rumors flew that St. Albans had been destroyed by southern soldiers.

As Vermonters organized to help the Union cause, political power became more concentrated in the state government. After the war was over in 1865, the stronger, centralized state government made it easier to raise money for improving highways and schools. At the same time, Vermonters held fast to their belief in the power of local government—especially the power of the town meeting.

A VERMONTER IN THE WHITE HOUSE

In 1881, as Vermont neared the end of its first hundred years as a state, the nation was shocked to hear the news that President James A. Garfield had been shot by an assassin only a few weeks after his inauguration. Nearly three months later he died, and his vice-president, Vermont-born Chester A. Arthur, was sworn in as president.

Arthur had made his political career in the state of New York, where he was an important member of the Republican party political machine. At that time, most government jobs were held by people appointed by influential members of the party. A reform movement was gathering support to establish a civil-service system for filling government offices. Because Arthur had been a part of the machine, many people expected him to oppose this reform, but he did not. He backed the Civil Service Act enthusiastically and administered it honestly.

During the manufacturing boom that took place in Vermont during the 1870s and 1880s, Brandon's Howe Scale Company prospered.

GROWTH OF INDUSTRIES AND CITIES

After the Civil War, agriculture in the state continued to decline. Many farmers moved to cities or bought better farmland in the Midwest. Thousands of Vermonters who served in the war chose not to return home. Instead, they took the federal government's offer of land in the West.

When Vermonters left the state in the late 1800s, immigrants took their places on the farms and in the factories and quarries. The Irish built the state's railroads. Quarry workers and stone cutters from Italy, Scotland, Sweden, Wales, and Spain came to work in the granite, marble, and slate quarries in Barre, Proctor, and Poultney. French Canadians settled in large numbers around the textile mills in Winooski. Miners from Cornwall, England, worked in the copper mines of Vershire and Ely.

During the 1870s and 1880s, Vermont's industries and cities experienced a growth spurt. The state's wood-processing and cheese-making industries expanded. Burlington became the third-

The falls and factories of Middlebury, about 1870

largest lumber mart in the country by importing timber from
Canada and exporting finished lumber to other cities in the
United States. St. Johnsbury's population tripled between 1830
and 1870 as manufacturing boomed. The scale factory built there
by Thaddeus Fairbanks, who invented the platform scale, spurred
this growth. Rutland became a railroading and manufacturing
center and saw its population triple. Springfield and Bellows Falls
were important centers of the machine-tool industry. Brattleboro
prospered as the home of the Estey Organ Factory. The insurance
industry flourished in Montpelier, with Julius Dewey's National
Life Insurance Company the largest of several companies.

While many Vermonters made their livings in enterprises other
than farming, none of those businesses employed enough workers
to create large cities in Vermont. The Industrial Revolution
brought changes to the state, but Vermont never became truly
industrialized. Huge cities with large factories did not develop. At
the end of the nineteenth century, Vermont remained mostly
rural, with the majority of its people living on farms.

Chapter 6
THE SECOND CENTURY

THE SECOND CENTURY

Vermont's centennial year, 1891, was marked by one event that probably seemed small at the time but was a significant portent of things to come. In that year, Vermont became the first state in the nation to officially encourage tourism by establishing a state publicity service. Twenty years later, in 1911, the service was enlarged and renamed the Bureau of Publicity. Its first publication was called "Vermont, Designed by the Creator for the Playground of the Continent."

THE SPANISH-AMERICAN WAR

For a few months in 1898, the United States was at war with Spain. The United States objected to Spain's harsh rule in Cuba and backed the Cuban independence movement. In February, the government sent the battleship *Maine* to protect Americans who were in Havana. When the ship was destroyed in an explosion, "Remember the Maine" became a popular slogan among those who favored war.

On March 17, United States Senator Redfield Proctor of Vermont gave a speech that described the terrible living conditions of the Cubans. Based on observations from a visit to Cuba, his speech caused more Americans to want war with Spain. In April, Congress declared war after much urging by President William McKinley.

Admiral George Dewey, of Montpelier, played a major role in ending the Spanish-American War by destroying the Spanish fleet in Manila Bay.

The Philippine Islands in the Pacific Ocean were also controlled by Spain. Commodore George Dewey, son of Julius Dewey of Montpelier, was put in command of the American Asiatic squadron. In May, he was ordered to attack the Spanish fleet in Manila. Dewey destroyed the fleet without the loss of any American lives. Two large cannons from one of the Spanish cruisers are displayed on the capitol lawn in Montpelier.

At the same time, another Vermonter, Captain Charles Clark, was ordered to sail the battleship *Oregon* from San Francisco to Santiago, Cuba. Clark made the 15,000-mile (24,140-kilometer) trip in sixty-six days. When Clark arrived in Santiago, he led the *Oregon* in the destruction of that Spanish fleet. The fighting ended in August, and a peace treaty was signed in December 1898. Cuba won its freedom, and Spain turned the Philippines over to the United States.

WORLD WAR I

Less then twenty years after the Spanish-American War, in April 1917, the United States entered World War I, which had started in August 1914 in Europe. Even before Congress passed the official declaration of war, Vermont's legislature had appropriated $1 million for war purposes.

During the war, about sixteen thousand Vermonters were in service, including almost two thousand men of the First Vermont Regiment. Admiral Henry T. Mayo, of Burlington, served as commander-in-chief of the Atlantic fleet. Altogether, 642 Vermonters died as a result of the war.

CALVIN COOLIDGE

On August 3, 1923, Calvin Coolidge became the second Vermont-born vice-president of the United States to rise to the highest office in the land.

Warren G. Harding, of Ohio, and Coolidge had been elected president and vice-president on the Republican party ticket in 1920. In the summer of 1923, Coolidge was on vacation at his parent's farm in Plymouth Notch, Vermont. News arrived by telegraph in the middle of the night that the president had died suddenly while on a speaking tour on the West Coast. Realizing that the country must not be without a president, Calvin's father, who was a notary, woke his son and administered the presidential oath of office to him. Because the farm had no electricity, the ceremony was conducted by the light of a kerosene lamp. When it was discovered that Coolidge's father did not really have the authority to swear in a federal official, Coolidge took the oath a second time from a judge in the District of Columbia.

Because the Coolidge family homestead in Plymouth Notch (right) had no electricity, Calvin's father administered the presidential oath of office by the light of a kerosene lamp.

Perhaps many of the popular ideas of what Vermonters are like grew out of President Coolidge's public image. He was a man of few words, sober in expression, and absolutely honest. Even though President Harding's administration had been full of scandal, none of it rubbed off on "Silent Cal." He won reelection easily in 1924. Times were good for many Americans in the 1920s, and the president got credit for what was called "Coolidge prosperity." Somewhat to his backers' surprise, Coolidge announced in 1927, "I do not choose to run for president in 1928."

THE FLOOD OF 1927

In November 1927, Vermont experienced the greatest natural disaster of its history. The month of October had been one of the rainiest on record, and more rain came on November 3 and 4. In many towns, the rivers overflowed their banks and rushed through the main streets. Many of the high-water marks left on buildings were well above the first floor. Houses were carried away, roads and railroads were ruined, and herds of cattle drowned. Eighty-five people died in the floods.

The state government went into high gear to repair the damage to highways, bridges, and public buildings. Before that time, Vermont's government had always operated on a "pay-as-you-go" policy. Now it became necessary to issue long-term bonds—and to accept federal assistance—to finance the needed public work.

THE GREAT DEPRESSION AND THE NEW DEAL

When the Great Depression hit the country in 1929, many Vermonters in rural areas hardly noticed. Making a living had never been easy in Vermont, and the prosperity of the 1920s had not really affected the state's economy. Sticking to their old voting pattern, Vermonters did not support the candidate who promised the country a New Deal.

From Civil War days on, Vermont was solidly behind the Republican party. When Democrat Franklin Delano Roosevelt was elected president of the United States in 1932 by a landslide electoral vote, Vermont's votes were not among them. Roosevelt went on to repeat the performance in three more elections, always without Vermont's support. In 1936, in fact, Roosevelt carried every state except Maine and Vermont.

Even though there was little popular support in the state for Roosevelt's New Deal programs, the severity of the Great Depression made it necessary for the state to accept certain kinds of federal assistance. One New Deal program furnished many long-term benefits to the state. The Civilian Conservation Corps (CCC) was set up to provide employment for underprivileged

During President Franklin Roosevelt's New Deal, CCC recruits were brought to Vermont to construct flood-control dams to prevent a repeat of the disastrous 1927 flood (above).

young men. Nearly forty-one thousand CCC recruits were brought into Vermont, where they planted forests; repaired bridges; built roads, parks, and ski slopes; and constructed flood-control dams to prevent a repeat of the 1927 disaster.

There were twenty-four CCC camps in Vermont, more than in any other state. Many of the young men were high-school dropouts from big cities who were experiencing outdoor rural life for the first time. A number of them managed to finish high school while in camp. The CCC men did a lot of good for Vermont, and the time they spent there was good for most of them, as well.

During the depression, in January 1934, an invention in Woodstock revolutionized Vermont's tourist industry. On a hill at Clinton Gilbert's farm, a rope tow powered by a Model "T" Ford engine hauled skiers uphill for the first time. A new era for winter sports and for Vermont's economy began.

In 1936, Vermont continued to show its independence of the federal government when it refused $18 million for construction of the Green Mountain Parkway. Running the whole length of the state with a highway, bridle path, and foot trail, it would have become a national park. In a referendum, Vermont's voters turned it down because Vermont would have had to give the federal government 35,000 acres (14,164 hectares) of land, which would have been administered by Congress.

WORLD WAR II

With the United States entry into World War II, the depression ended. Vermont's General Assembly actually declared war in September 1941, three months before the attack on Pearl Harbor led to Congress's declaration of war. Here's how it happened.

President Roosevelt had called the National Guard into service, and an infantry regiment from Vermont went into training in the spring of 1941. Some members of the state legislature wanted to give their servicemen a state bonus, in addition to their federal pay. This had always been done in wartime, but there was no legal basis for doing it when the country was officially at peace.

In September, the president issued orders to the United States Navy to return fire if they were attacked at sea. When this occurred, the Vermont General Assembly adopted a declaration that a state of "armed conflict" existed, and then passed the state bonus for their National Guardsmen. Newspapers carried the story that Vermont had independently declared war.

Nearly 50,000 Vermonters served in the various branches of service during World War II; 1,233 of them lost their lives. Thousands of others left the state, taking trains south to work for the war effort in the factories of Massachusetts and Connecticut.

Shelburne Shipyards was active, building torpedo patrol boats for the war in the Pacific. Machine tools for the war effort were shipped from Springfield. Along with the rest of the nation, Vermonters concentrated all their efforts on bringing the war to a victorious end.

A NEW POPULATION BOOM

In 1940, the United States had nearly eight times as many people as it had a hundred years earlier. Vermont's total, however, had increased by only 69,000 people, about 23 percent.

After World War II, the situation changed. The postwar baby boom, plus newcomers from other states and countries, gave the state an increase of 15,000 people in just five years. The trend continued, and the fifty years between 1940 and 1990 saw a growth equal to that of the state's first fifty years.

New industries such as electronics and computer manufacturing brought in some of the newcomers. Others came as a result of a "back-to-the-land" movement in the 1960s and 1970s. Thousands of young people chose to find a quieter, more fulfilling life in rural areas. Vermont's small towns, its lovely scenery, and its reputation for tolerance of individualism had great appeal. Some who came found that the problems they confronted were greater than the rewards and did not stay. Others stayed and started small businesses.

The most important factor in Vermont's rapid growth was a huge expansion of recreational facilities. Dozens of developers and thousands of their clients became convinced that this state was, indeed, designed to be the "Playground of the Continent," just as the Bureau of Publicity had claimed years earlier. Not everyone approved of unrestricted development, however.

Widespread construction of ski trails, condominium developments, resorts, and vacation homes on the Green Mountains' slopes had brought new growth and prosperity to the state in the postwar years. It also had brought problems. Concern for protection of the natural environment was a popular topic of discussion and debate.

Farms were being subdivided for vacation homesites, and real estate prices were soaring. With more people came the demand for more roads, more electricity, and more public services. Vermont's clear streams and lakes were threatened with pollution.

ENVIRONMENTAL LEGISLATION

Governor Deane C. Davis and the state legislature decided it was time to do something to protect the state's environment. Legislation was needed, they decided, to put the brakes on uncontrolled development. In 1970, the General Assembly passed the Environmental Control Law, based on a phrase from the state's constitution:

> Private property ought to be subservient
> to public uses when necessity requires it.

No state had ever done anything like this before. The Environmental Control Law put the rights of the public squarely ahead of the rights of developers, just as the framers of the state constitution had said they should be.

The new law stated that permits are required for any substantial development, public or private. The developer or subdivider has to submit evidence to prove that a proposed project would have no adverse effect on the surroundings. The law also provided that a Land Capability Plan would be drawn up and that all new development would have to comply with the plan. In addition, the law calls for the governor to appoint district environmental commissions to examine and pass on all new projects, and for a state environmental board to act as a court of appeals above the district commissions.

RECENT DEVELOPMENTS

In 1988, the legislature passed another act designed to go even further in its efforts to control the state's growth and development wisely. The Growth Management Act of 1988 gives communities both the authority and the resources to draw up plans for land use within their jurisdictions. Towns and agencies are required to hold public hearings on the plans and to encourage the public to participate. These plans can be used to protect open land, save critical natural resources and environmental areas, and preserve historic landmarks. They can also be used to aid good development and promote affordable housing.

Under the Growth Management Act, funds were allocated for the Housing and Conservation Trust Fund and for two programs of aid to farmers.

In 1989, Governor Madeleine Kunin signed a law that will prohibit air conditioning in cars after 1993. Any automobile manufacturers who continue to use chlorofluorocarbons (CFCs) — which damage the ozone layer — in the air-conditioning systems of their cars will not be able to sell their cars in Vermont.

In recent years, Vermonters have started taking better care of their forests. When Champlain first came into the region, nearly 90 percent of the land was covered with forests. Much of the tree cover was cut during the nineteenth century to create pastureland for sheep. Today, the proportion of forestland has risen again to

As part of Vermont's effort to preserve the environment, Governor Madeleine Kunin (left) in 1989 signed a law that will prohibit air conditioning in cars after 1993.

nearly 80 percent. Vermont is a far more attractive and ecologically balanced state today than it was a hundred years ago.

Not all Vermonters believe that recent environmental legislation is totally good for the state. They fear the increased concentration of power in the hands of the state and away from the towns. Some criticize it as antibusiness or antigrowth; others argue that growth is not always a good thing.

Vermont's recent legislation grew out of a sincere desire to preserve the state's natural environment, something most Vermonters have always wanted to do. The passage of these laws certainly proves one thing—that people of this rocky, hilly, "backwoods" little state are no more afraid of taking controversial positions today than their founding fathers were in 1777. One way or another, Vermonters will find a way to keep the clear air and scenic beauty of their Green Mountain state. After all, those are the qualities that the people of Vermont have always revered.

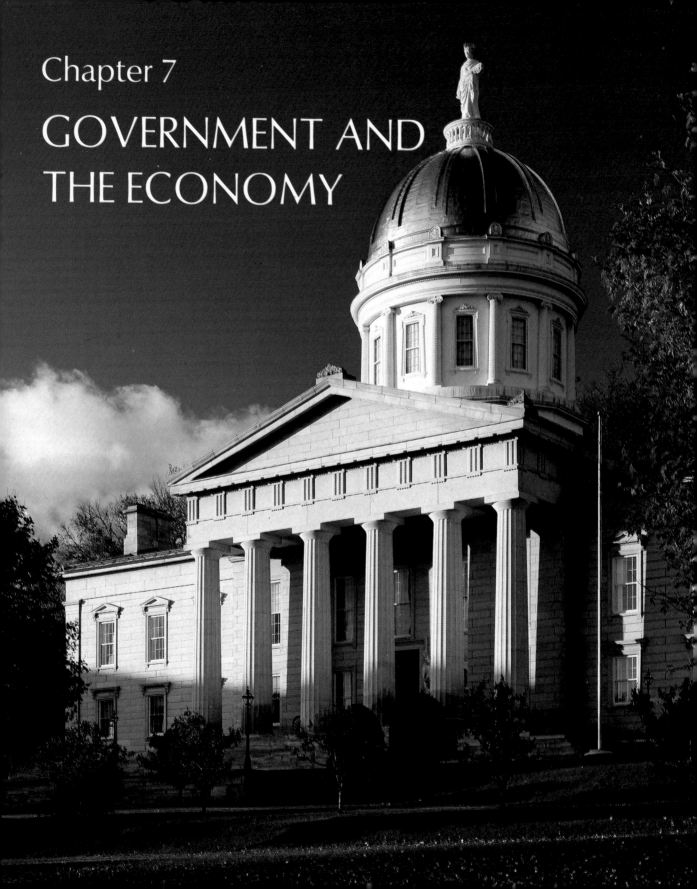

Chapter 7
GOVERNMENT AND THE ECONOMY

GOVERNMENT AND THE ECONOMY

Vermont is governed by the state's original constitution, adopted in 1777 and revised in 1786 and 1793. The present constitution has been amended many times. Final approval for any amendment must come from a majority of the voters.

About half of Vermont's revenue comes from taxes, such as the state income tax, general sales tax, and taxes on public utilities, tobacco products, and motor fuels. Federal grants and programs provide most of the other half of the state's income.

GOVERNMENT

The government of Vermont, like that of most other states, is divided into three branches: executive, legislative, and judicial. Each branch has its own special functions.

The executive branch is headed by the governor. This official, along with a lieutenant governor, a treasurer, a secretary of state, an attorney general, and an auditor of accounts, are elected for two-year terms. The governor has the power to commission all officers of government and—with the approval of the senate—to fill every vacancy in any office that occurs because of death or other reasons. Other powers include the authority to grant pardons, to execute laws, to draw funds from the treasury for purposes authorized by the General Assembly, to grant licenses as directed by law, to call special sessions of the legislature, and to direct the state's military forces.

Vermont's legislature is the General Assembly, which consists of a 30-member senate and a 150-member house of representatives. Senators and representatives serve two-year terms. The two houses enact laws for the state. Bills relating to revenue must originate in the house; constitutional amendments must begin in the senate. The General Assembly is scheduled to convene in odd-numbered years, in January, but usually meets in even-numbered years also.

The judicial branch is headed by a supreme court consisting of a chief justice and four associate justices. The supreme court has administrative control of the superior, county, probate, and district courts of the state.

Justices of the supreme court and the ten judges of the superior court are elected by the legislature for six-year terms. The governor appoints district court judges. All other assistant judges and judges of probate are elected by the people to four-year terms.

Vermont's government is geared toward active participation by the citizens of the state in two ways. First, state officials are elected for only two years, rather than four, as in most other states. This means the people have the opportunity to elect new representatives more often. Second, the legislature is large in proportion to the population of the state, meaning that the voters can easily contact their representatives to voice their opinions.

All citizens of the United States aged eighteen or over are eligible to vote in Vermont's elections, regardless of how long they have lived in the state. However, according to the state constitution, they must also be "of a quiet and peaceful behavior," and they have to pledge to be good citizens by taking the historic "freeman's oath," which follows:

You solemnly swear (or affirm) that whenever
you give your vote or suffrage, touching any
matter that concerns the State of Vermont, you
will do it so as in your conscience you shall
judge will most conduce to the best good of
the same, as established by the Constitution,
without fear or favor of any person.

TOWN MEETINGS

Politically and geographically, Vermont is divided into 242
towns—called townships in most other states—and 9 cities. The
state also has 3 gores—odd-shaped pieces of land left over by early
surveyors who were laying out town boundaries. They are
isolated, hard to get to, and have been uninhabited, for the most
part, from the beginning of the state's history.

The town is a very important entity in Vermont. A city or
village within a town may become incorporated and make many
decisions for itself, but farmers and others who live outside the
village or city limits may have their say each March at the annual
town meeting. Citizens of each town gather together in their town
hall. Every adult, male or female, rich or poor, educated or not,
has the right to be heard on any subject that is brought up. Topics
are discussed, debated, and voted on.

The official agenda usually includes electing officials, approving
budgets, and debating local issues such as whether or not to build
a new bridge or a new school. World issues also are sometimes a
matter of intense debate. In 1982, 177 Vermont towns passed
resolutions that instructed their United States senators and
representative to work for a nuclear freeze. The citizens of
Vermont believe in using their town meetings to make their
feelings known on any vital subject. They thoroughly believe that

The University of Vermont, in Burlington (left), and Bennington College, in Bennington (right), are among the state's institutions of higher education.

grass-roots democracy has its finest hours during town meetings. Here people can voice their opinions and vote their conscience directly, in addition to writing letters to their elected representatives.

Until quite recently, Vermonters successfuly resisted pressure to centralize government powers, believing that most issues are best handled at the local level. Whatever happens in the future, Vermont would be changed forever if town meetings were to end.

EDUCATION

As early as the New Hampshire Grants period, education was important in Vermont. In 1761, the town of Guilford voted to fund a public school. Vermont's 1777 constitution required each town to provide a public school. Today, there are about 93,000 students enrolled in Vermont's 395 public elementary and secondary schools. Currently, a state law requires that students from the ages of seven through fifteen attend school.

There are seventeen colleges and universities in Vermont. The oldest is the University of Vermont, in Burlington. It was founded in 1791, the year Vermont became a state. There are three state colleges, at Castleton, Johnson, and Lyndonville.

Among the state's private colleges are Bennington College, in Bennington; Champlain College, in Burlington; Goddard College, in Plainfield; Marlboro College, in Marlboro; Middlebury College, in Middlebury; St. Michael's College, in Winooski; Trinity College, in Burlington; and Vermont College of Norwich University, in Montpelier.

Several Vermont colleges offer specialized training. The School for International Training in Brattleboro is a four-year college for young people planning to work in jobs overseas. It grew out of the Experiment in International Living, a student exchange program based in Putney. The New England Culinary Institute, based in Montpelier with a branch program in Essex Junction, trains students of all ages for work as chefs, restaurant managers, and in the field of hotel food services. Norwich University, in Northfield, is one of the country's leading military schools, and Vermont Law School, in South Royalton, trains lawyers.

MANUFACTURING

Manufacturing provides the major source of Vermont's income through the production of over $2 billion worth of products a year. Employing 21 percent of Vermont's workers, manufacturing contributes 26 percent of the gross state product (GSP) — the total value of goods and services produced in the state each year. Vermont's businesses tend to be small in size, however. As of

Vermont's manufactured products include markers made of granite from the Rock of Ages quarry (left) and headstones made by the Vermont Marble Company (right).

1988, fewer than 150 employers had more than 100 people on their payrolls. Only two companies—General Electric and IBM—had more than 2,000 employees.

Vermont has a highly diversified manufacturing base. Drills, grinders, lathes, and other machine tools are still made in Springfield and Windsor. Burlington serves as the production center for hand tools and military weapons. Production of paper and paper products, which takes place throughout the state, is the state's most important wood-processing industry.

In recent years, high-tech industries in Burlington and Essex Junction have begun turning out electronic equipment, computers, computer components, and computer software. Other important manufactured products include furniture; fishing rods; hockey sticks; marble memorials and tile; and stone and granite markers, memorials, and tombs.

Tourism and leisure-time activities bring Vermont about $700 million each year.

SERVICE INDUSTRIES

Vermont's service industries account for 62 percent of the GSP. About 67 percent of the state's workers are employed in wholesale and retail trade; finance, insurance, and real estate; community, social, personal, and government services; and transportation, communication, and utilities.

The state's large cities and tourist areas have the most service industries. Burlington is a financial center, and Montpelier, the state capital, is the center for government services. The wholesale trade of Vermont's dairy products, machinery, and stone products is important to the state's economy.

Tourism and leisure-time activities provide the largest income— about $700 million—of the service industries and make up the second-most important segment of the state's economy, after manufacturing. Vacationers have always come to Vermont in the summer to enjoy the cool mountain breezes, the back roads, and wilderness activities such as hiking, camping, and fishing. Since the invention of the rope tow in 1934, the skiing industry has turned several tiny mountain villages into major tourist resorts. Hotels, motels, restaurants, and real estate companies selling vacation homes and condominiums in these areas employ thousands of workers.

AGRICULTURE

While Vermont is mostly rural, it is no longer mostly agricultural. Agriculture's importance to the state's economy is only a fraction of what it once was. It produces only about 1 percent of the GSP and employs only 6 percent of Vermont's workers. Dairy farming is the most important agricultural pursuit in Vermont. About 80 percent of the money earned in the state from agriculture comes from dairy products. While the number of dairy farms, farmers, and cows has been dropping ever since World War II, the size of farms and their productivity have increased. In 1950, the average dairy farmer had a herd of ten cows; by 1982, the average had increased to more than sixty.

Even though manufacturing and tourism have passed dairy farming in importance to Vermont's economy, the production of milk and dairy products is still vital to the consumers of New England. About 40 percent of all dairy production in the New England region comes from Vermont.

A good portion of milk from Vermont's dairy farms is used for the manufacture of cheese. Farmers' cooperatives, notably the seventy-year-old Cabot Farmers' Cooperative Creamery, have made Vermont cheeses famous. Another Vermont dairy product—

Dairy farming is the most important agricultural pursuit in Vermont.

Ben and Jerry's Ice Cream—has zoomed its way into wide popularity across the country. It was first made in a small ice cream store in Burlington.

Livestock—cattle, hogs, sheep and lambs, and poultry—accounts for another 10 percent of Vermont's agricultural earnings; maple products, 3 percent; and other crops, such as potatoes, apples, corn, hay, and oats, 7 percent.

MAPLE PRODUCTS

Vermont is the country's leading producer of maple syrup. While maple products do not bring in a large portion of the total dollars earned in Vermont, they are prized by gourmets and are widely recognized symbols of the state. Many a Vermont resident remembers with fondness the unique taste of each spring's first

Vermont is the country's leading producer of maple products.

offering of "sugar on snow." An old-fashioned treat, it consists simply of hot syrup poured onto a plate of clean snow (or onto a snowbank). The cold temperature of the snow turns the hot syrup into a soft, delicious taffy.

Maple syrup production is a long and labor-intensive enterprise. When the first thaw signals the end of winter, sap rises in trees. In sugar maples, found all over Vermont, the sap contains a small amount of natural sugar. For generations, farmers have tapped the trees. That is, they drive a small spout, called a spile, through the outer trunk. A bucket is hung below the spile, and the sweet sap drips through the spile and into the bucket.

The next step in the process is to transport the sap through the woods to the sugarhouse. This used to be done by oxen- or horse-drawn sledges. Today, some sugarbush groves have networks of plastic tubing that carry the sap.

Next, the sap must be boiled down to the consistency of syrup, or even longer to create maple sugar or candy. It takes ten gallons of sap to produce one gallon of syrup. No wonder pure Vermont maple syrup is expensive!

MINERAL RESOURCES

The mining and quarrying industry, once a dominant sector of the state's economy and one that brought thousands of immigrant workers to settle there, has shrunk to a tiny producer of jobs. At last count, it employed fewer than five hundred workers.

Today, granite is the state's most valuable mineral product. Quarries near Barre are the largest in the United States. Rutland County produces slate; Windham and Windsor counties, talc; and Chittenden County, limestone. Marble deposits are located in the west-central part of the state, near Proctor. Other mineral deposits include asbestos, sand, and gravel.

TRANSPORTATION

About 14,000 miles (22,530 kilometers) of roads and highways wind through the Green Mountain state, with the interstate highway system making up 320 miles (515 kilometers). Interstate 91 crosses Vermont north to south, from the Canadian to the Massachusetts borders. For most of the route, it parallels the Connecticut River. Interstate 89 runs northwest from White River Junction at the New Hampshire border to Montpelier and Burlington and then north to Canada. State and federal highways, as well as ferry routes across Lake Champlain, lead to New York.

There are about one hundred covered bridges along Vermont's roads—more than in any other state. These include railroad

Among Vermont's more than one hundred covered
bridges are one over Black Creek near Perkinsville
(top left), a railroad bridge in Wolcott (top right),
a bridge at Clare (right), and one that spans the
Quechee Gorge River near Taftsville (above).

bridges and bridges on public and private lands. The longest covered bridge spans the Connecticut River between Windsor, Vermont, and Cornish, New Hampshire. The longest one within the state is the Scott Covered Bridge in West Townshend, which is 276 feet (84 meters) long and has three spans. The oldest is the Pulp Mill Covered Bridge, built around 1820 in Middlebury. In the early 1900s, iron and steel started to replace wood for building bridges. After that, covered bridges were not built except to replace historic structures. The newest covered bridge was built in the early 1980s, in Rockingham, to replace one ruined by a truck. There are four covered bridges near Northfield Falls.

Between 1849 and 1910, Vermonters laid about 1,100 miles (1,770 kilometers) of railroad track. Since then, the amount of track has decreased to about 737 miles (1,186 kilometers). Currently, Amtrak passenger lines serve seven Vermont cities, and twelve freight lines operate throughout the state. Vermont has about twenty airports, including Burlington International Airport, the state's chief air terminal.

COMMUNICATION

The *Burlington Free Press* has the largest circulation of Vermont's newspapers. Other newspapers with large circulations include the *St. Albans Messenger*, the *Barre-Montpelier Times-Argus*, and the *Rutland Herald*, Vermont's oldest continuously published newspaper—since 1794. Altogether, Vermont has about thirty newspapers, ten of which are dailies.

Vermont's first radio station, WSYB, began broadcasting in Rutland in 1930. The state's first television station, WCAX-TV, went on the air from Burlington in 1954. Today, Vermont has about forty radio stations and seven television stations.

Chapter 8

ARTS AND RECREATION

ARTS AND RECREATION

Vermonters are likely to think of themselves as pragmatic and practical, but they also prize the arts—literature, art, music, and theater. When not hard at work, residents of the Green Mountain State enjoy outdoor recreation and special fairs and festivals available throughout Vermont.

LITERATURE

Ethan and Ira Allen have an important place in Vermont's literary heritage as well as in its political history. During the New Hampshire Grants controversy, Ethan wrote many pamphlets upholding the rights of Vermont's original settlers. In 1779, Ethan published an account of his captivity with the British during the Revolutionary War. *Reason, the Only Oracle of Man*, published in 1784, gave Ethan and Vermont a reputation for godlessness because it placed reason ahead of faith and religion. Ira wrote a history of the state, as well as the preamble to Vermont's 1777 constitution.

Thomas Rowley of Danby wrote poems and songs whose political themes inspired the Green Mountain Boys. Royall Tyler, author of the first American comedy performed regularly before audiences, wrote many novels after he moved to Vermont in 1790. Through the characters in his works, Tyler portrayed the Yankee characteristics still associated with Vermont.

Poet Robert Frost (right) was a founder of the Bread Loaf School of English (left).

In the early 1800s, Daniel P. Thompson wrote enormously popular historical novels, of which *The Green Mountain Boys* is considered the best. During the 1880s and 1890s, Rowland E. Robinson captured Vermonters' stories, manners, habits, and ways of speaking in several books of essays and anecdotes. Rudyard Kipling, a well-known English writer, married a Vermont woman and lived in Dummerston from 1892 to 1896. During those years, Kipling wrote his famous *Jungle Book* and *Captains Courageous.*

During the twentieth century, other writers from many states and foreign countries have made their homes in Vermont. Poet Robert Frost is one of the best-known of these literary figures. Born in 1874 in San Francisco, he lived in New England from the age of ten, finally settling in Vermont. Many of Frost's poems, such as "Mending Wall" and "Stopping by Woods on a Snowy Evening," are about life in rural New England.

Frost was one of the founders of the Bread Loaf School of English, affiliated with Middlebury College and located in Ripton.

He served on the faculty of several colleges even though he never earned a college degree. Among the many honors conferred on Robert Frost were the 1923, 1930, 1936, and 1942 Pulitzer Prizes in poetry and more than forty honorary degrees. In 1960, the United States Congress voted him a gold medal in recognition of his poetry, and the following year the state legislature named him poet laureate of Vermont.

Dorothy Canfield Fisher, a contemporary of Robert Frost, was born in Kansas but spent most of her adult life in Arlington. She wrote popular stories and novels about everyday family life. In addition, she wrote about the state for the Vermont Bureau of Publicity.

Sinclair Lewis, author of the best-selling novels *Main Street* and *Elmer Gantry* in the 1920s, was living in Barnard when he received the Nobel Prize in literature in 1930. His book *It Can't Happen Here* had a Vermont setting. Dorothy Thompson, Lewis's wife, was a syndicated newspaper columnist and author of several books. Barnard was her home from the 1930s until her death.

Perhaps the most famous resident of Vermont today is Aleksandr Solzhenitsyn, the Russian novelist and historian. In 1974, the Soviet Union exiled this 1970 winner of the Nobel Prize in literature because of his criticism of the Soviet system. Moving to the United States in 1976, Solzhenitsyn settled on a farm near Cavendish, where he continues to write.

ART

Vermont has also been home to several artists and architects. Hiram Powers of Woodstock gained the nation's attention in 1843 with his statue *Greek Slave*. His bust of John Marshall and statues of Benjamin Franklin and Thomas Jefferson are in the Capitol in Washington, D.C. Altogether, he sculpted more than 150 busts of famous historical figures.

Two sets of artist-architect brothers—the Meads and the Hunts—lived in Brattleboro. In 1856, Larkin Mead's snow sculpture *Recording Angel*, done in Brattleboro, brought him into the public eye because snow sculpturing was unusual at that time. Later, he did permanent versions of *Recording Angel* in marble. Mead's statues of Ethan Allen in the state capitol and in Statuary Hall in the nation's Capitol and the Lincoln Memorial in Springfield, Illinois, are his best-known works.

Architect William Mead, Larkin's younger brother, designed the capitol of Rhode Island and the Boston Public Library. From 1909 to 1927, he served as the president of the American Academy at Rome. Richard Morris Hunt, another architect from Brattleboro, designed luxurious homes in Rhode Island and New York for the Vanderbilts and John Jacob Astor. Hunt's public works include the Tribune Building in New York, the base of the Statue of Liberty, and the National Observatory in Washington, D.C.

Hunt's older brother, William, was a celebrated artist who studied in France and opened a school of painting in Boston. His murals in the New York capitol are his best-known works. William Hunt is perhaps more important for encouraging the French artist Jean François Millet when Millet was ridiculed by French critics. Millet's *The Angelus, The Sower,* and *The Reaper* are now world famous.

Thomas Waterman Wood had the greatest effect on Vermont art. In 1895, he established the Wood Gallery of Art in Montpelier. Besides his self-portraits and paintings depicting Vermont life, the gallery displays the works of contemporary Vermont artists. Wood's well-known painting *The Contraband, Recruit and Veteran,* which depicts blacks, hangs in the Metropolitan Museum of Art in New York.

During the twentieth century, Vermont's most famous resident artist was Norman Rockwell, who was originally from New York. Rockwell spent many years in Arlington, where he used native Vermonters as models for his *Saturday Evening Post* covers.

THE PERFORMING ARTS

The Vermont Symphony Orchestra is different from symphony orchestras in large cities. Its members come from many different towns and several states, so getting together for rehearsals takes unusual effort and dedication. Concerts are presented in various locations, too, to give all the people in the state the opportunity to hear them. Summer concerts are held outdoors. The Vermont

Norman Rockwell, Vermont's
most famous resident artist,
often used local people
as models for his *Saturday
Evening Post* covers.
The Christmas Day, 1948,
issue also included
Rockwell himself (with pipe)
and New York primitive
artist Grandma Moses (at
left with glasses and cameo).

Symphony is the oldest state-supported symphony in the United States.

In Brattleboro, a group of nonprofessional singers named the Blanche Moyse Chorale has become known far and wide for the quality of its work. The chorale has appeared on national television and has traveled to give concerts in this and other countries. An immigrant from Switzerland, Blanche Moyse is also the founder of the New England Bach Festival at the Brattleboro Music Center. She has trained local people from different occupations and interests to make beautiful music together.

Jazz festivals are staged at some of the ski resorts in the summer. Summer concerts of different types of music are given in Burlington, Craftsbury, Derby Line, Stowe, and at the Adamant

Cross-country skiing and mountain climbing are popular activities in Vermont.

Music School near Montpelier. At other times of the year, concerts are scheduled in several locations including Burlington, Montpelier, and St. Johnsbury. In Marlboro each summer, Marlboro College hosts the Marlboro Music Festival, which features chamber music. The Vermont Mozart Festival presents outdoor concert series in summer and chamber music in winter.

Vermont's theater groups include the Vermont Repertory Theater and St. Michael's Playhouse, both in Winooski, and the Mad River Playhouse in Waitsfield.

The Onion River Arts Council in Montpelier, Barre Opera House in Barre, Catamount Arts in St. Johnsbury, Johnson Friends of the Arts in Johnson, the Millhouse Bundy Performing and Fine Arts Center in Waitsfield, the Flynn Theatre for the Performing Arts in Burlington, and the Lane Series sponsored by the University of Vermont schedule performances of music, opera, theater, and dance during different seasons. Among other towns, Dorset and Weston are locations for summer theater productions.

SPORTS

As one would expect in a state where fields and yards are covered with a thick blanket of snow for at least four—and sometimes six—months of the year, winter sports have always been popular in Vermont. Skating, sledding, tobogganing, sleigh riding and racing, hockey, ice fishing, and especially skiing are enjoyed throughout the state. Vermont boasts 1,800 miles (2,897 kilometers) of cross-country ski trails. There are thirty resorts for alpine (downhill) and nearly sixty for Nordic (cross-country) skiing. Most resorts feature skiing classes for people at all skill levels and all ages.

With lakes in nearly every town in the state, Vermonters and visitors enjoy sailing, canoeing, swimming, fishing, and water-skiing. Canoeing has been popular on the lakes and rivers of Vermont since the days when American Indians used birchbark canoes as a major means of transportation. Today, guided canoe trips are popular with tourists in the state. Ferry rides across Lake Champlain and scenic shoreline cruises out of Burlington give passengers a chance to enjoy this large freshwater lake.

Hiking—from casual strolls in the woods to serious long-distance treks—gets people out into some of the most beautiful and unspoiled parts of the state. Vermonters take hiking very seriously. In 1910, a number of outdoor enthusiasts decided there should be a trail along the backbone of the state so that hikers could enjoy the whole stretch in safety. They organized the Green Mountain Club, and over the next twenty years marked the 262-mile (422-kilometer) Long Trail from a point near Jay Peak on the Canadian border to an exit into Massachusetts near Pownal. Shelters were built along the way for overnight stops; they are available to all hikers on a first-come, first-served basis. The Long Trail is said to be three to four weeks long and about two hours wide. In other words, it can easily be hiked in three to four weeks, and one is never more than a two-hour hike from "civilization."

Bike touring—trips of more than a day by bicycle—is also popular with tourists who join an organized group and take to the road. Since there are few level stretches in Vermont, most of the ride is spent either pumping uphill or coasting down. Modern mountain bikes make this easier than it once was.

A less strenuous activity is driving around the countryside. Viewing the scenery, especially the fall foliage, and driving through some of Vermont's one hundred covered bridges is an activity enjoyed by thousands of visitors each year.

Although Vermont has no professional sports teams, many Vermonters follow the New York, Massachusetts, and Canadian teams. Local high school and college teams also have many fans.

FAIRS AND FESTIVALS

Throughout the year, Vermont cities and villages host fairs and festivals. These events celebrate Vermont's seasons, art, music, or history, and some are just for fun. Middlebury College's Snow Bowl, Brattleboro's Winter Carnival, and Poultney's Snow Fest revel in the lighter side of winter. Sugar-on-snow, sour pickles, and raised doughnuts are gobbled up by sugarhouse visitors during the April Maple Sugar Festival in St. Albans. During the Fourth of July weekend, families take part in three-legged races and watch water-skiing competitions and fireworks at St. Albans Bay Day. Each September, Rutland hosts the Vermont State Fair.

Vermonters of all ages enjoy riding a fire truck during the Bethel Autumn Festival.

Children perform concerts and attend workshops during the Yellow Barn Music Festival each July in Brattleboro. September brings the Old Time Fiddlers' Contest to Barre and the State Championship Fiddlers' Contest to Bellows Falls. Also in September, Stratton Mountain hosts the Arts Festival, which features paintings, photographs, and crafts. The craft of quilt making is honored at the Vermont Quilt Festival in Northfield each July. The Mount Snow Foliage Craft Fair in October exhibits pottery, jewelry, glass, and weaving.

Horses are the center of attention at the Killington Mountain Equestrian Festival in July when five hundred horses and riders compete for $110,000 in prize money. A pony pull, a horse show, and livestock judging are featured at the Deerfield Valley Farmers Day Exhibition each August in Wilmington.

The state's history is honored during the July Lake Champlain Discovery Festival. In August, Old Home Days in Rockingham celebrates the founding of the town's meetinghouse with dancing, a car rally, and fireworks. Stratton Mountain's Wurstfest in September pays tribute to the area's German heritage in a festival of German food and music.

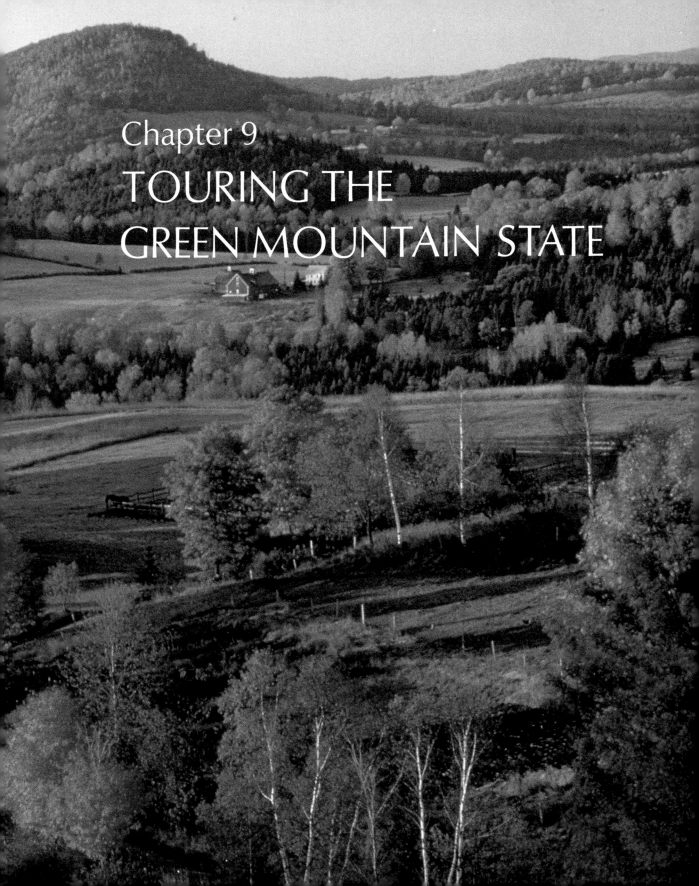

Chapter 9
TOURING THE
GREEN MOUNTAIN STATE

TOURING THE GREEN MOUNTAIN STATE

Tourists in Vermont are not always people from out of state. Many residents, too, enjoy exploring the highways and back roads, winding around the curves and up and down the hills, and following the rivers. In fact, there is an organization of about five thousand members called the 251 Club. The number refers to the 242 towns and 9 cities in the state, and the objective of all members is to visit every one of those geographic spots. One is a "minus" member until reaching that goal, after which he or she becomes a "plus" member.

In autumn, brilliant displays of fall foliage that spread across the hills and valleys are the main attraction for visitors to the state. Highways are jammed and country inns are filled with "leaf peepers," as the locals call them. Winter brings the skiers and winter sports fans.

Spring ushers in the "sugar season," when the sweet, sticky smell of boiling maple sap fills the air. More than 150 maple sugarhouses in the state are open to the public in season, and visiting one is a real treat.

In summer, people tour Vermont to enjoy the scenery of mountains and meadows, rivers and lakes, and pretty little towns. Dozens of villages, centered on a green, are filled with houses, churches, country inns, and town halls that have been there since the late 1700s. Scenic overlooks, lovely lakes, waterfalls, and picturesque covered bridges can easily be found around almost every bend. Our tour of Vermont concentrates on historic sites and truly unusual things to see or do.

Two towns in southwestern Vermont are Manchester (far left) and Bennington, with its historic Battle Monument (left).

SOUTHWESTERN VERMONT

Bennington, in the southwestern corner of the state, was the site of the Catamount Tavern where Ethan Allen and the Green Mountain Boys met and planned the raids on British forts at Ticonderoga and Crown Point. Today, a plaque marks this historic site. In the Old Bennington Historic District, a street leading up to the Bennington Battle Monument is lined with fine examples of eighteenth-century homes. A 306-foot (93-meter) limestone shaft commemorates the Battle of Bennington, an important encounter with the British in 1777 when the Green Mountain Boys achieved lasting fame.

Bennington College, one of the finest—and most expensive— liberal-arts schools in the country, is located here, as is Bennington Potters, makers of famous top-quality dinnerware.

The Bennington Museum has a complete collection of Bennington pottery and collections of Early American glass and furniture. One of its most valuable possessions is the oldest Stars and Stripes in existence. The museum also contains a collection of paintings by the famous artist Grandma Moses and the schoolhouse she once attended, which was moved here from its original site in New York.

Arlington, north of Bennington, for fourteen years was the home of artist Norman Rockwell. Many of the local residents served as his models for magazine covers and illustrations. Some of them serve as guides in the Arlington Gallery, where many of Rockwell's original paintings, illustrations, and other works are displayed.

Farther north, Manchester was a popular destination for wealthy "summer people" in the 1800s. The famous Equinox House, recently restored, was one of the grandest resorts in all of New England. Hildene, at the edge of town, was the twenty-four-room summer home of Robert Todd Lincoln, son of President Lincoln. It is filled with Lincoln family furnishings and possessions. The beautiful hillside estate of 400 acres (162 hectares) includes a formal garden and a carriage house. The Big Bromley and Stratton Mountain ski areas are a short drive from town. At Big Bromley, there is summer sledding on the Bromley Alpine Slide. Another favorite summer activity is riding the scenic chair lift to the top of the mountain and back. Five states can be seen from the summit.

SOUTHEASTERN VERMONT

Brattleboro is the cultural and economic center of southeastern Vermont. As the nearest major town in the state to Boston, it has always appealed to writers and others who want to escape the city, but not too far. Fort Dummer, the first settlement in the state, was 2 miles (3 kilometers) south of town. The Brattleboro Museum and Art Center houses a permanent collection of organs manufactured by Jacob Estey in Brattleboro. Just west of Brattleboro is Marlboro, home of the Marlboro Music Festival. Dummerston, to the northwest, hosts a huge Apple Pie Festival each fall.

Putney, north on the Connecticut River, is the home of the Putney School, one of the nation's most highly regarded preparatory schools. Santa's Land, a Christmas theme park open from May to Christmas, has exhibits, an iceberg slide, sleigh and hay rides, a sleigh museum, and a petting zoo.

Farther north on the Connecticut River is Bellows Falls, once a major railway center. During the summer, excursion trains operating from town to Chester Depot and Ludlow give passengers a taste of what train travel in this scenic area was once like. Rock carvings done hundreds of years ago by the Penacook Indians can be seen near the falls.

To the northwest is Chester, a village with several stone houses that were built by Scots from Aberdeen. Many of them are said to have secret rooms that served as stations on the Underground Railroad in the mid-1800s. Runaway slaves were sheltered there as they escaped to freedom in Canada.

Still farther northwest is Weston, site of the state's first town meeting. Weston has two country stores, a fine summer theater, and the Kinhaven Music School. Free concerts are presented every weekend during the summer. On Sundays, many visitors attend services at the Weston Priory and hear choral music sung by Benedictine monks.

Due east, on the Black River, lies Springfield, often called the birthplace of the machine-tool industry. The falls of the Black River powered many early factories. The oldest schoolhouse in the

Vermont's first constitution was adopted at the Old Constitution House in Windsor (left). Brattleboro (right) is the cultural and economic center of southeastern Vermont.

state, the Eureka Schoolhouse built in 1790, was recently restored. A collection of Bennington pottery, Richard Lee pewter, and nineteenth-century carriages, clothing, dolls, and paintings are displayed at the Springfield Art and Historical Society.

On the Connecticut River north of Springfield is Windsor, called the "Birthplace of Vermont." The Old Constitution House, where seventy-two delegates adopted Vermont's first constitution in July 1777, is preserved and open to the public. Housed in an 1846 armory and machine shop, the American Precision Museum displays many Yankee inventions such as rifles, typewriters, and engines. Windsor's Vermont State Craft Center exhibits works by Vermont's artisans.

Plymouth Notch, up in the mountains west of Windsor, was the birthplace and childhood home of President Calvin Coolidge. Visitors can visit the farmhouse and see where his father swore him into office as president.

WEST-CENTRAL VERMONT

Rutland is Vermont's second-largest city and the site of the annual Vermont State Fair. Marble and slate quarries in the vicinity brought thousands of workers to the area early in this century. The Norman Rockwell Museum, with more than two thousand pictures and other items from the illustrator's career, is located in Rutland. The Pico Alpine Slide, east of Rutland, has a chair lift that takes passengers to the top of the slide.

Southeast of Rutland, in Cuttingsville, visitors can observe ironworking in a large blacksmith shop. Vermont Industries, Inc., also has a museum of old blacksmithing equipment and a company store.

North of Rutland is Proctor. The town is named for Redfield Proctor, who built a successful marble company and also served the state as governor and as a United States senator. In 1922, the Vermont Marble Company had seventy-five quarries and produced 1 million cubic feet (28,317 cubic meters) of marble. Vermont marble was used for many of the important buildings and monuments in Washington, D. C., as well as in other countries. Today, the Vermont Marble Exhibit is open to the public. Displays explain how marble is formed, and artisans demonstrate the process of finishing and carving it. Wilson Castle, a nineteenth-century mansion with carved mahogany paneling, ceilings stenciled in gold leaf, and eighty-four stained-glass windows, is just outside Proctor.

Several maple museums in the state reflect the importance that maple syrup has played in Vermont's history. One claiming to be the world's largest is in Pittsford, north of Proctor. To the west is Hubbardton Battlefield, scene of the only battle of the Revolutionary War fought on Vermont soil.

Wilson Castle (left), a nineteenth-century mansion near Proctor, has eighty-four stained-glass windows. The Morgan Horse Farm near Middlebury (above) breeds Morgan horses.

Due north is Middlebury, home of Middlebury College, the Johnson Art Gallery, and the Sheldon Museum. The Sheldon Museum has a collection of everyday household objects relating to nineteenth-century Vermont. The Vermont State Craft Center at Frog Hollow, which holds classes and workshops, features the work of local artisans. Changing exhibits and video shows illustrating traditional Vermont folk art are presented at the Vermont Folklife Center, in the middle of town. The Middlebury Inn, on the square, is an outstanding example of the state's many old and lovely inns.

A few miles southeast of Middlebury is Ripton, one-time home of poet Robert Frost. His cabin can be toured by appointment. Nearby is the famous Bread Loaf School and Writers Conference, where Frost once taught. Chimney Point, west of Middlebury at Lake Champlain, was an early French settlement. The Chimney Point Tavern, built in 1784, is preserved as an eighteenth-century taproom, open to the public in summer. Just north of Middlebury is the University of Vermont's Morgan Horse Farm, a breeding center for Vermont's own Morgan horses.

Quechee Gorge is known as Vermont's Little Grand Canyon.

EAST-CENTRAL VERMONT

Woodstock, a well-known resort town, is the home of the Vermont Institute of Natural Science. Birds of prey live here in huge cages at the institute's Raptor Center. Woodstock is also the site of the first rope tow to carry skiers uphill. Just north of Woodstock is Billings Farm and Museum, an operating dairy farm with exhibits of Vermont farm life in the nineteenth century. Farther north is Quechee Gorge, a 1-mile- (1.6-kilometer-) long chasm known as Vermont's Little Grand Canyon. Not very large, its fame lies in its spectacular beauty.

To the east lies White River Junction, where the White River meets the Connecticut. Once a major railroad center, the town is still a major transportation center because Interstates 89 and 91 intersect there.

Interstate 89, which runs northwest to Burlington, ranks among the most scenic interstate highways in the nation. From White River Junction it passes Sharon, where a tall granite monument commemorates the birthplace of Mormon founder Joseph Smith;

South Royalton, home of Vermont Law School; Randolph, where Vermont Technical College is located; and Northfield, site of Norwich University, the nation's oldest private military school.

Interstate 91 follows the Connecticut River for the southern part of its route through the state. Off the highway west of Fairlee, many summer camps for boys and girls are located on the shores of Lake Fairlee. Also west of town is Lake Morey, named for Vermonter Samuel Morey, who invented the steamboat.

THE NORTHEAST KINGDOM

The Northeast Kingdom is a name invented by former United States Senator George Aiken to refer to three Vermont counties—Essex, Orleans, and Caledonia. The least populated region of this sparsely populated state, these three counties have 27 percent of the state's area but less than 11 percent of its people. The largest town, St. Johnsbury in Caledonia County, has fewer than eight thousand people. There are very few towns at all in Essex County, which has a total population of only about sixty-six hundred. This county is almost entirely wilderness, with deep, clear lakes, rugged mountain slopes, and thick forests.

Tourism, however, is alive and thriving at the ski areas of Jay Peak and Burke Mountain and along the shores of Lake Willoughby. In the summer and during the peak of the fall foliage season, a sixty-passenger aerial tramway takes passengers to the top of Jay Peak, near the Canadian border. Interstate 91 cuts through the heart of the kingdom, from south of St. Johnsbury to Derby Line at the Canadian border, making many small towns much more accessible than they once were.

The Fairbanks Museum and Planetarium in St. Johnsbury, founded in 1889, has more than 100,000 objects relating to natural

Glover's annual Bread and Puppet Domestic Resurrection Circus features a mock circus and a puppet show with giant-sized puppets.

science, technology, regional history, and the arts. Even older is the St. Johnsbury Athenaeum, founded in 1871 and said to be the oldest art gallery maintained in its original condition in the United States. Located at the east edge of town, the Maple Grove Maple Museum and Factory is the world's largest factory for the processing of maple syrup and sugar.

West of St. Johnsbury, in Cabot, is the Cabot Farmers' Cooperative Creamery, a major producer of Vermont's famous cheddar cheese. Visitors can see the cheese being made and watch a video about Vermont's dairy industry.

Heading north, thousands of people find their way to the little town of Glover each summer to attend the annual Bread and Puppet Domestic Resurrection Circus. A free show, it includes a mock circus and an outdoor puppet show with giant-sized puppets. The Bread and Puppet Theater and Museum there is open during the summer.

Above: Waterbury's Ben & Jerry's Ice Cream Factory trucks dispense sandwiches as well as ice cream.
Right: The Vermont Historical Society Museum in Montpelier is housed in a century-old red-brick hotel.

NORTH-CENTRAL VERMONT

Barre is the granite center of the world. The Rock of Ages quarry gives visitors the chance to view the huge pit that has yielded fine stone for hundreds of the world's great buildings, and hundreds of thousands of gravestones and monuments. A train ride takes people right into the quarry to watch the stone being dug out and hoisted to the surface. In the huge crafts center, master carvers turn the rough stone into works of art. Hope Cemetery is a showcase for some of the finest work of Barre granite sculptors and carvers.

To the north is Montpelier, the smallest capital city in the United States, with 8,241 people. Its graceful State House, made of Vermont granite, sits in front of a rounded, tree-covered hillside. Rising above the Greek-style portico, supported by six Barre granite columns, is a gold-leaf dome. Near the State House is the

Vermont Historical Society Museum and research library, housed in a century-old red-brick hotel. Three miles (5 kilometers) from the capital is the Morse Farm Sugar House, with sugarhouse tours and a slide show.

Two businesses worth visiting in Waterbury, to the northwest, are the Cold Hollow Cider Mill and Ben & Jerry's Ice Cream Factory. At the mill, visitors watch a documentary movie about cider and maple products and view the process of cider making. Ben & Jerry's lets visitors observe how their famous ice cream is made and offers free samples at the end of the tour.

Stowe, north of Waterbury, is known around the world as a ski capital. The town has done a good job of keeping its own traditional look, despite growth and prosperity. Mount Mansfield, Vermont's highest peak, and Spruce Peak are the area's main attractions. A four-passenger gondola carries skiers in winter and sightseers in summer to the top of Mount Mansfield. Drivers can reach the top via a toll road. There is a giant alpine slide, which operates in the summer, on nearby Spruce Peak.

Smugglers Notch, near Mount Mansfield, is so named because of the smuggling of goods into Canada that took place during the War of 1812. The narrow cut through the rocky mountainside is picturesque. Visitors drive, bike, and hike to the notch, and rock climbers scale the bluffs beside the highway.

THE CHAMPLAIN VALLEY

Ferry rides across Lake Champlain are favorite summer jaunts. Boats leave on regular schedules from Charlotte, Vermont, to Essex, New York; from Burlington, Vermont, to Port Kent, New York; and from Grand Isle, Vermont, to Plattsburgh, New York. Passengers are treated to great views of both the Green Mountains and the taller Adirondacks on the New York side of the lake. Highways link the mainland with the lake's main islands, Grand Isle and Isle La Motte.

The Vermont Wildflower Farm in Charlotte is a summer spectacular, with 6 acres (2.4 hectares) of natural gardens, woodlands, and ponds. There is also a wildflower seed shop.

Shelburne, home of the Shelburne Museum, is halfway between Charlotte and Burlington. Collections of folk art and artifacts and American and European paintings are housed in thirty-seven historic buildings. A lighthouse and the steamship *Ticonderoga*, located on the museum's grounds, commemorate the history of the lake. One could spend days there without seeing everything. At Shelburne Farms, visitors ride in an open wagon past nineteenth-century farm buildings, stroll through gardens, enjoy views of the lake and the Adirondacks beyond, and watch a show about the history of the farm.

Burlington, to the north, is Vermont's largest city and home of the University of Vermont. Summer brings the Vermont Mozart Festival and the Champlain Shakespeare Festival, concerts by the Vermont Symphony Orchestra, and several performing-arts series to the city. The *Spirit of Ethan Allen*, a replica of the sternwheelers that used to cruise Lake Champlain, makes several daily excursions on the lake. Recreational facilities include golf courses, tennis courts, health clubs, and public beaches on Lake Champlain. Joggers, walkers, and bikers enjoy a path along the lake. In the winter, downhill and cross-country skiing are just minutes away. The Robert Hull Fleming Museum, on the campus of the University of Vermont, houses a splendid collection of American and European art.

To the east, the Discovery Museum in Essex Junction features hands-on science, history, and art exhibits geared to the interests

Cosmos at the Vermont Wildflower Farm

of children. At its outdoor facility, injured and orphaned native animals are nursed and cared for.

Due north is St. Albans, a railroad town and center of dairying and maple syrup production. The Franklin County Museum houses memorabilia from the town's smuggling days during the War of 1812, of its history as a stop on the Underground Railroad, and as the site of the northernmost conflict during the Civil War.

Isle La Motte, to the northwest, is a village on the island of the same name in Lake Champlain. It was here that the French first settled in 1666 and constructed a fort. St. Anne's Shrine commemorates the first mass celebrated in Vermont. A large granite statue of Samuel de Champlain honors his discovery of the lake in 1609.

The tour of the state ends where Vermont's history began. As Vermont starts its third century, it faces many challenges. Without a doubt, its citizens will meet these challenges with the same courage, determination, and imagination that has been displayed by all generations of Vermonters since the days of the Green Mountain Boys.

FACTS AT A GLANCE

GENERAL INFORMATION

Statehood: March 4, 1791, fourteenth state

Origin of Name: The state's name is derived from the French words *vert* (green) and *mont* (mountain).

State Capital: Montpelier

State Nickname: Green Mountain State

State Flag: The state flag features the state coat of arms on a field of dark blue. The coat of arms has a pine tree, three sheaves of grain, a cow in a pastoral setting, and mountains in the background. A stag's head appears above the enclosed landscape. The state name and motto and crossed pine branches are at the bottom of the coat of arms.

State Motto: Freedom and Unity

State Bird: Hermit thrush

State Flower: Red clover

State Tree: Sugar maple

State Animal: Morgan horse

State Fish: Brook trout (cold water); walleye pike (warm water)

State Insect: Honeybee

State Butterfly: Monarch butterfly

State Beverage: Milk

State Song: "Hail Vermont!" words and music by Josephine Hovey Perry, adopted as the state song in 1938:

Hail to Vermont! Lovely Vermont!
Hail to Vermont so fearless!
Sing we a song! Sing loud and long!
To our little state so peerless!
Green are her hills, Clear are her rills,
Fair are her lakes and rivers and valleys;
Blue are her skies, Peaceful she lies,
But when roused to call she speedily rallies.

Proud of Vermont, Lovely Vermont,
Proud of her charm and her beauty;
Proud of her name, Proud of her fame,
We're proud of her sense of duty;
Proud of her past, Proud first and last,
Proud of her lands and proud of her waters;
Her men are true, Her women too.
We're proud of her sons and proud of her daughters.

Hail to Vermont! Dear old Vermont!
Our love for you is great.
We cherish your name,
We laud! We acclaim!
Our own Green Mountain State.

Hail to Vermont! Dear old Vermont!
Our love for you is great.
We cherish your name,
We laud! We acclaim!
Our own Green Mountain State.

POPULATION

Population: 511,456, forty-eighth among the fifty states (1980 census)

Population Density: 53 people per sq. mi. (20 people per km^2)

Population Distribution: According to the 1980 census, Vermont had the highest percentage of rural population of the fifty states, about 66 percent. The rural population increased 12 percent between 1970 and 1980; the urban population increased 21 percent.

Burlington	37,712
Rutland	18,436
South Burlington	10,679
Barre	9,824
Bennington	9,349
Brattleboro	8,596
Montpelier	8,241
Essex Junction	7,033
Winooski	6,318
Springfield	5,603
Newport	4,756

(Population figures according to 1980 census)

Population Growth:

Year	Population
1790	85,425
1800	154,465
1810	217,895
1820	235,981
1830	280,652
1840	291,948
1850	314,120
1860	315,098
1870	330,551
1880	332,286
1890	332,422
1900	343,641
1910	355,956
1920	352,428
1930	359,611
1940	359,231
1950	377,747
1960	389,881
1970	444,732
1980	511,456

GEOGRAPHY

Borders: The shape of Vermont resembles a wedge, wide and flat at the top and narrower at the bottom. The northern boundary of the state is the Canadian province of Quebec. On the east, the Connecticut River separates Vermont from New Hampshire. The state borders Massachusetts on the south. New York State is the western boundary, with part of the line going through Lake Champlain.

Highest Point: Mount Mansfield in the Green Mountains, 4,393 ft. (1,339 m)

Lowest Point: Lake Champlain in Franklin County, 95 ft. (29 m)

Greatest Distances: North to south, 158 mi. (254 km)
East to west, 97 mi. (156 km)

Area: 9,614 sq. mi. (24,900 km^2)

Rank in Area Among the States: Forty-third

National Forests: The Green Mountain National Forest covers 325,534 acres (131,740 hectares) along the backbone of the Green Mountains.

The Connecticut River near Newbury

Rivers: The longest river within the state's borders is Otter Creek, which—along with the Winooski, Lamoille, and Missisquoi rivers—flows into Lake Champlain. The White, Black, and West rivers flow into the Connecticut River.

Lakes: The state's largest lake is Lake Champlain on the western border, of which about 60 percent is in Vermont. Other lakes include one-third of Lake Memphremagog, on the northern border, and Bomoseen, Willoughby, Carmi, St. Catherine, and Seymour lakes.

Topography: The most prominent topographical region of Vermont is the Green Mountains, which extend north to south from the Canadian border to the Massachusetts state line. The Green Mountains are the oldest mountains in New England, formed more than 500 million years ago by the uplifting and buckling of the earth's crust. The Green Mountains' highest peaks are over 4,000 ft. (1,219 m). Slow erosion by wind, water, and glacial ice have formed and shaped Vermont's landscape. A much lower range, the Taconic Mountains, straddles the Vermont-New York border. Near the New Hampshire border are the isolated series of peaks of the Northeast Highlands. Prominent valleys include the Champlain Valley, between Lake Champlain and the Green Mountains; the narrow Valley of Vermont, to the north of the Taconic Mountains; and the Vermont Piedmont, a narrow corridor of hills and valleys east of the Green Mountains.

Climate: Vermont's temperatures vary with the altitude. Winters are generally colder and the summer nights cooler in the higher elevations of the Green Mountains. The average January temperature is 17° F. (-8° C). The average July temperature is 68° F. (20° C). The record high temperature of 105° F. (41° C) was registered at Vernon on July 4, 1911; the record low was -50° F. (-46° C) on December 30, 1933, at Bloomfield. The average annual precipitation is 39 in. (99 cm). The average annual snowfall ranges from 60 to 80 in. (152 to 203 cm) in the lower altitudes and from 80 to 120 in. (203 to 305 cm) in the mountains.

NATURE

Trees: Maples, ashes, beeches, birches, oaks, elms, tamaracks, pines, spruces, firs, hemlocks, cedars

Wild Plants: Gentians, asters, bloodroots, Dutchman's-breeches, lupines, trilliums, jack-in-the-pulpits, pitcher plants, bog orchids, and Solomon's seals

Animals: White-tailed deer, coyotes, red foxes, snowshoe hares, raccoons, squirrels, woodchucks, porcupines, bears, beavers, otters, moose, skunks, lynxes

Birds: Ravens, gray or Canada jays, saw-whet owls, orioles, cardinals, chickadees, robins, finches, grosbeaks, woodpeckers, nuthatches, hummingbirds, bluebirds, martins, quails, geese, loons, pine martens, thrushes

Fish: Perch, several species of trout, bream, eel, salmon, catfish, sheepshead, carp

GOVERNMENT

Vermont has three branches of government—executive, legislative, and judicial. Executive officials include the governor, lieutenant governor, treasurer, secretary of state, auditor of accounts, and attorney general—each elected to a two-year term. The executive branch, headed by the governor, administers the law. The governor has the authority to veto or approve the laws passed by the General Assembly. However, the General Assembly can override the governor's veto if two-thirds of the senate and two-thirds of the house approve the bill. The governor is also empowered to grant pardons and call together the General Assembly, when necessary. The governor is the commander-in-chief of the state militia.

The legislative branch—the General Assembly—consists of a 150-member house of representatives and a 30-member senate. All legislators are elected to two-year terms. The state is divided into 13 senatorial districts and 106 representative districts.

The judicial branch interprets the laws and tries cases. The five justices of the supreme court and the ten judges of the superior court are elected by the legislature. They hold office for six-year terms. Assistant judges, judges of probate, and state's attorneys are elected by the people for four-year terms.

Town meetings are held on the first Tuesday in March. Citizens of each of Vermont's 251 towns and cities—which are similar to the townships of other states—elect their town officials, determine the town's budget, and make decisions on items of local interest.

Any person eighteen years of age or older, who is eligible to be a voter in Vermont, is also eligible to run for any public office, including state representative, state senator, lieutenant governor, and governor.

Number of Counties: 14

U.S. Representatives: 1

Electoral Votes: 3

Voting Qualifications: Eighteen years of age, citizen of the United States; no minimum residency requirement

Vermont Law School, at South Royalton

EDUCATION

Vermont law requires that students from ages seven through fifteen attend school. The state's elementary and secondary public school system includes about 395 schools with about 93,000 students.

The University of Vermont, founded in 1791 in Burlington, is the oldest institution of higher education in the state. Middlebury College, organized in Middlebury in 1800, is Vermont's oldest private college. Norwich University in Northfield, founded in 1819, is the oldest private military college in the United States. Other colleges and universities include state colleges in Castleton, Johnson, and Lyndonville; Bennington College and Southern Vermont College, both in Bennington; Burlington College, Champlain College, and Trinity College, in Burlington; College of St. Joseph, in Rutland; Goddard College, in Plainfield; Green Mountain College, in Poultney; Marlboro College, in Marlboro; St. Michael's College, in Winooski; School for International Training, in Brattleboro; Vermont College of Norwich University, in Montpelier; and Vermont Law School, in South Royalton.

ECONOMY AND INDUSTRY

Principal Products:

Agriculture: Cattle, sheep, horses, milk and dairy products, corn, hay, apples, maple syrup and sugar, potatoes, Christmas trees, nursery products

Manufacturing: Electric and electronic equipment, computers and computer components, scales and measuring devices, machine tools, lumber and wood products, paper and paper products, food and food products, printing and publishing, stone and marble products

Natural Resources: Granite, marble, slate, sand and gravel, crushed stone, talc, asbestos

Business: Service industries account for 62 percent of the gross state product (GSP) and employ about 67 percent of the state's workers. Of the service industries, tourism provides the largest income—about $700 million a year. Manufacturing, however, is the state's major source of income, producing over $2 billion worth of products a year. Agriculture, once the state's most important source of income, contributes only 1 percent of the GSP today.

Communication: Vermont's newspaper with the largest circulation is the *Burlington Free Press*. Other newspapers with large circulations are the *Rutland Herald*—the state's oldest continuously published newspaper—the *St. Albans Messenger*, and the *Barre-Montpelier Times-Argus*. Vermont has about thirty newspapers, ten of which are dailies.

Transportation: Vermont's first railroad, completed in 1849, served mainly as a link to Boston and not as intrastate transportation. That railroad soon went into receivership, as did other state lines. From the high of nearly 1,100 mi. (1,770 km) of track in 1910, the trackage has shrunk to 737 mi. (1,186 km).

The highway system of 14,000 mi. (22,530 km) includes state and town roads as well as 320 mi. (515 km) of interstate highways. Interstate 91 traverses the state from the Canadian border on the north to Massachusetts on the south, paralleling the Connecticut River most of the way. Interstate 89 connects Burlington with the Canadian border on the north and runs southeast from Burlington to Montpelier and then through White River Junction near the border of New Hampshire. In the west, state and federal highways lead to New York. One links islands in Lake Champlain to the mainland in both states. There are also three ferry routes across the lake.

Burlington International Airport is the state's major air terminal. There are about twenty other airports in the state.

SOCIAL AND CULTURAL LIFE

Museums: Vermont's many museums reflect the history of the state and the varied interests of its citizens. The Vermont Historical Society, in Montpelier, has collections from prehistoric times to the present, with permanent and temporary exhibits. In Manchester, the American Museum of Fly Fishing has a collection of fly-fishing equipment, plus tackle used by famous Americans such as Daniel Webster and President Dwight D. Eisenhower. The American Precision Museum in Windsor houses a collection of tools and their products, including tools used by Thomas Edison and products made by Henry Ford. The Bennington Museum has an extensive collection of Bennington pottery, works of art by Grandma Moses, historical artifacts, and American glass. Brattleboro Museum and Art Center, located in the town's former Union Railroad Station, has a variety of art and exhibits a collection of Estey organs manufactured in Brattleboro. Housed in a former dairy barn, The Bread and Puppet Museum of Glover includes the puppets, masks, and theater materials used by the Bread and Puppet Theater. Essex Junction's Discovery Museum is a children's museum with hands-on exhibits, live animals, and an art gallery. In St. Johnsbury, Fairbanks Museum and Planetarium features natural and cultural history, presents seasonal shows in the planetarium, and includes an official U.S. weather station that has been in operation since 1894. The Norman Rockwell Museum in Rutland features more than 2,000 items of Rockwell paintings, illustrations, and memorabilia, including the complete series of the artist's *Saturday Evening Post* covers.

Libraries: Vermonters have always prized books and libraries. Vermont's first library was started in Brookfield in 1796. A list of 255 libraries was published by the state department of libraries in 1989. The list included college and museum libraries, as well as those established for the general public. None of the public libraries was donated by the Carnegie Foundation, as were so many others in the nation. Many of Vermont's own philanthropists established memorial libraries; others were set up by the citizens of the towns.

The largest academic collection in the state is the University of Vermont's more than 779,000 volumes. The Vermont Historical Society has a large collection of state and local history manuscripts—including a complete collection of town histories—8,000 broadsides, maps, photographs, and the largest genealogy reference library in the state. One of the most unusual collections to be found anywhere is at the Proctor Free Library. The Proctor family owned the marble quarries where many new immigrants were employed. Emily Proctor collected a large number of children's books in the native languages of these immigrants, so that young people who had not yet completely mastered English would have interesting books to read in their own language. Her donations also included foreign-language books for adults.

Performing Arts: Music and summertime go together in Vermont. Among the state's events are the Marlboro Music Festival at Marlboro College, the New England Bach Festival at Brattleboro, the Vermont Mozart Festival in Champlain, jazz festivals at the ski resorts, and concerts of various kinds of music throughout the state. Concerts are not limited to summertime; many are scheduled throughout the year in Burlington, Montpelier, St. Johnsbury, and other cities. Vermont also has a statewide, state-supported symphony orchestra and the Blanche Moyse Chorale, located in Brattleboro.

Theater productions are presented at the Flynn Theatre for the Performing Arts, in Burlington; at the Vermont Repertory Theater and St. Michael's Playhouse, both in Winooski; and at the Mad River Playhouse in Waitsfield. Other theater groups are active in Montpelier, Barre, Dorset, and Weston.

Sports and Recreation: Winter sports on the snow and ice are popular in Vermont. These include downhill and cross-country skiing, skating, sledding, tobogganing, hockey, and ice fishing. Summer sports such as canoeing, sailing, swimming, fishing, camping, biking, and hiking attract people to Vermont's lakes, woods, and hills. The Green Mountain National Forest and the thirty-one state parks, six state forests, and various recreation areas are favorite places to enjoy Vermont's summer and winter outdoor activities.

Historic Sites and Landmarks:

Bennington Battle Monument, in Bennington, is the tallest structure in Vermont and one of the tallest battle monuments (306 ft./93 km) in the world. The

Equinox House, in Manchester, was one of New England's grandest resorts and a popular destination for "summer people" in the 1800s.

monument commemorates the Battle of Bennington (actually fought in New York State), where colonial forces defeated a British expedition on August 16, 1777.

Calvin Coolidge Birthplace and Homestead, within the Plymouth Historic District of nineteenth- and early twentieth-century buildings, is the boyhood home of the thirtieth president of the United States.

Chester A. Arthur Birthplace, in Fairfield, is a replica of the birthplace of the twenty-first president of the United States. A brick church where Arthur's father preached is nearby.

Equinox House, in Manchester, is the grande dame of Vermont's historic nineteenth-century resort hotels. The public rooms of the white-columned inn are furnished in Victorian style; the oval dining room with its sky-blue vaulted ceiling faces Mount Equinox.

Ethan Allen Homestead, in Burlington, is the 1787 farm of the organizer of the Green Mountain Boys.

Eureka Schoolhouse, in Springfield, the oldest schoolhouse in the state, was built in 1790. This one-room schoolhouse is one of the few remaining eighteenth-century public buildings in Vermont.

Hildene, in Manchester, is the twenty-four-room summer home of Robert Todd Lincoln, Abraham Lincoln's son. His descendants used the house until 1975. Original family furnishings, personal memorabilia, and an Aeolian pipe organ add to the interest of this house.

Hubbardton Battlefield and Museum, near Hubbardton, became the site of the only Revolutionary War battle fought on Vermont soil when colonial troops in retreat from Fort Ticonderoga delayed the British and Hessian forces on July 7, 1777.

Hyde Log Cabin, in Grand Isle, is considered to be the oldest existing log cabin in the nation. Built in 1783, it was restored by the Vermont Board of Historic Sites in 1956. The cabin is furnished with eighteenth-century artifacts.

Justin Smith Morrill Homestead, in Strafford, was built between 1848 and 1851 by Senator Morrill, the father of the Land-Grant College Act. The seventeen-room "cottage" is one of the finest examples of a Gothic revival house in Vermont.

Old Constitution House, in Windsor, is now a museum devoted to Vermont history. In 1777, the first state constitution of Vermont was written and signed there.

Old First Church, in Bennington, was built in 1805. The oldest graveyard in Vermont, adjacent to the church, contains the grave of poet Robert Frost as well as the graves of those who died in the Battle of Bennington.

Old Stone House Museum, in Brownington, is housed in a thirty-room, four-story, granite-block 1830s building originally used as a dormitory for schoolchildren. It was built by the Reverend Alexander Twilight, the first black legislator in America. Exhibits include kitchen tools, needlework, art, and furniture from nineteenth-century Vermont.

Rokeby Museum, in Ferrisburgh, built about 1784, was the home of Rowland T. Robinson, an abolitionist who used the house as a station on the Underground Railroad.

Shrine of St. Anne, in Isle La Motte, is on the site of Vermont's first European settlement, Fort St. Anne, built in 1666. The shrine commemorates the site of the first mass in Vermont.

Smugglers Notch, between Stowe and Jeffersonville, is a mountain pass that was used by Vermonters during the War of 1812 to hide cattle and other supplies prior to smuggling them into Canada for the British army.

State Capitol, in Montpelier, completed in 1859, was built of Barre granite in the Doric style. The dome is covered with gold leaf. Inside the portico stands a statue of Ethan Allen and a brass cannon captured from the Hessians in the 1777 Battle of Bennington.

Stellafane Observatory, in Springfield, has been designated a National Historic Landmark because of its pioneering role in the development of popular astronomy and amateur telescope making in the United States. Since the construction of the clubhouse and observatory in 1924 and 1930, respectively, the buildings have remained in continuous use.

Billings Farm and Museum, in Woodstock

Other Interesting Places to Visit:

American Precision Museum, in Windsor, is housed in the former Robbins and Lawrence Armory. Exhibits include machine tools and their products and show the use and development of the various tools.

Arlington Gallery's Norman Rockwell Exhibition, housed in a nineteenth-century church in Arlington, contains examples of the artist's work, including a collection of *Saturday Evening Post* magazine covers.

Ben & Jerry's Ice Cream Factory, in Waterbury, has tours that include a slide show telling the story of how Ben and Jerry started making their ice cream in 1978. At the end of the tour, a visit to the ice cream parlor features free samples of the Ben & Jerry's flavors.

Bennington Potters, in Bennington, offers a tour of the pottery factory that produces stoneware, dinnerware, terra cotta, art sculptures, planters, and other pottery.

Billings Farm and Museum, in Woodstock, is a living-history museum and working dairy farm that depicts life in nineteenth-century Vermont.

Bromley Alpine Slide, on Bromley Mountain near Manchester, is a speed-controlled sled ride open during the summer. The descent winds for nearly 1 mi. (1.6 km) through woods and meadows. From the top of the chair lift there is a spectacular five-state view.

Fairbanks Museum and Planetarium, in St. Johnsbury, is a mosaic of nature and culture founded in 1889 by Franklin Fairbanks, a naturalist and scientist. The towered, Romanesque structure of red sandstone is in the National Register of Historic Buildings. This is also an official U.S. weather station and the home of the Northern New England Weather Center.

Green Mountain Audubon Nature Center, in Huntington, is a 230-acre (93-hectare) sanctuary with trails through many typical Vermont habitats, including beaver ponds, a hemlock swamp, a sugar orchard, and old farm fields.

Green Mountain Railroad, between the railroad stations in Bellows Falls and Chester, offers sightseeing trips aboard a 1935 diesel train. On the two-hour trip, the train goes through three river valleys.

Joseph Smith Birthplace Memorial, in Sharon, marks the site of the Mormon prophet's birth. The story of the founder of the Church of Jesus Christ of Latter-day Saints is presented through paintings, sculptures, exhibits, and films in two buildings on the grounds. A monolith of Barre granite is engraved with the dates of Smith's birth and death.

Maple Grove Maple Museum, in St. Johnsbury, offers tours through the world's largest candy factory. The Old Sugar House demonstrates the process of boiling down maple sap to make sugar and syrup.

Morse Farm Sugar Shack, near Montpelier, specializes in maple syrup. The sugarhouse is in full operation during March and April, but the sugaring-off process may be seen any time of the year.

Norman Rockwell Museum, in Rutland, houses more than 2,000 items of Rockwell memorabilia spanning sixty years of the artist's career, including the complete series of *Saturday Evening Post* covers.

Quechee Gorge, near Quechee, is Vermont's "Little Grand Canyon." The Ottauquechee River forms the 165-ft.- (50-m-) deep gorge. The bridge on U.S. Route 4 spans the gorge and offers a good view of this natural spectacle.

Rock of Ages, near Barre, is one of the world's largest granite quarries. From the pinnacle of the quarry, visitors can watch the quarriers carve mammoth blocks from the quarry, then lift the 100-ton (91-metric-ton) blocks with derricks. From the observation deck of the Craftsman Center, visitors can see the granite-manufacturing plant in full operation.

Shelburne Farms, near Shelburne, is a 1,000-acre (405-hectare) agricultural estate built in the 1880s as the summer residence of Dr. William Seward Webb and his wife, Lila Vanderbilt Webb. The grounds, landscaped by Frederick Law Olmstead and forested by Gifford Pinchot, once totaled 3,800 acres (1,538 hectares). Farming, cheese making, and furniture making are among the activities engaged in on the estate.

Shelburne Museum, in Shelburne, is a village of thirty-seven buildings that was created in 1947 by Electra Havemeyer Webb as a place to house and share her vast collection of Americana, which includes carriages, sleighs, and the sidewheeler SS *Ticonderoga.* The grounds are enhanced by perennial flower gardens, including one of the finest lilac gardens in New England.

Sheldon Museum, in Middlebury, houses a large collection of nineteenth-century "Vermontiana." There are hand-forged kitchen utensils, both country and formal furniture, oil portraits, toys, and a carpenter's workshop.

Vermont Institute of Natural Science, in Woodstock, was founded in 1972 and is dedicated to environmental education and natural-history research. Of special interest is the Vermont Raptor Center, a unique living museum that houses twenty-six species of owls, hawks, and eagles. These raptors, or birds of prey, are permanently injured and unable to survive in the wild.

Vermont Marble Exhibit, in Proctor, explains how marble is formed, quarried, and finished into works of art or for use in homes and public buildings. Visitors can watch a sculptor at work, visit a sculpture gallery, and view a film about marble.

Vermont State Craft Center at Frog Hollow, in Middlebury, displays the work of more than 250 Vermont craftspeople in a restored mill overlooking Otter Creek Falls.

Wilson Castle, near Proctor, built in 1867, is a thirty-two-room house that features stained-glass windows, fireplaces with imported tiles, and antique furnishings.

IMPORTANT DATES

10,000 B.C.—Archaeological finds suggest the presence of pre-Algonquian group settlements along Otter Creek

A.D. 1300-1750—The Algonquian and Iroquois use the Vermont region for hunting grounds, fishing, and gathering, with large permanent settlements and agriculture

1609—Samuel de Champlain, the first European explorer to arrive in the area, claims the Vermont region for France

1666—The French build and briefly occupy Fort St. Anne on Isle La Motte

1690—The English build a fort at Chimney Point

1724—English colonists from Massachusetts build the first permanent white settlement at Fort Dummer, near present-day Brattleboro

1731—The French build a fort at Crown Point in New York

1741—The king of England gives the Vermont region to New Hampshire

1749—Bennington is the first town chartered by Governor Benning Wentworth in the Vermont region that came to be known as the New Hampshire Grants

1759—The Crown Point military road is built across the region from Springfield to Crown Point; Robert Rogers leads an expedition that destroys the villages of the St. Francis Indians in Canada

1763—The French and Indian War ends and England takes control of Vermont

1764—New York gains jurisdiction over Vermont when the British crown extends New York's northeast boundary to the Connecticut River, overriding New Hampshire's claims to the area

1770—New York courts rule that landholders in the Vermont region must have New York land grants or lose their land; Ethan Allen organizes the Green Mountain Boys and scares off defenseless settlers with New York titles, flouting the New York courts

1775—Ethan Allen and the Green Mountain Boys capture Fort Ticonderoga from the British in the Revolutionary War; Allen is captured by the British in Montreal

1776—American forces, under Benedict Arnold, are defeated in a naval battle on Lake Champlain

1777—Vermont declares itself an independent state with the name New Connecticut; the settlers adopt the present name, Vermont, and a new constitution; a Vermont contingent routs a detachment under British General Burgoyne at the Battle of Bennington

1778—The first election under the Vermont constitution is held; Thomas Chittenden is chosen as the first governor; Ethan Allen is released by the British and returns to Vermont

1785—The first marble quarry in the United States is started at East Dorset by Isaac Underhill

1786—A constitutional convention adopts major revisions of the Vermont constitution

1790—The first U.S. patent, signed by George Washington, is issued to Samuel Hopkins of Pittsford for making potash out of wood ashes; the boundary dispute with New York is settled

1791—Vermont gives up its status as an independent state and becomes the fourteenth state to be admitted to the Union; the University of Vermont is chartered

1793—The nation's first copper mine is established at Strafford; a constitutional convention revises the 1788 Vermont constitution, which becomes the foundation for all subsequent constitutional amendments; Samuel Morey operates a steamboat on the Connecticut River from Fairlee; the first Bennington pottery is made

1802 — The first canal built in the United States begins operation at Bellows Falls

1805 — Montpelier is chosen as the state capital; a charter is issued for the town of Sterling, the last grant of unappropriated land in the state; Joseph Smith, founder of the Church of Jesus Christ of Latter-day Saints, is born in Sharon

1808 — The legislature meets at Montpelier for the first time in the newly completed state capitol; Vermont's first fire-fighting society is chartered

1814 — The first school of higher education for women is established by Emma Willard at Middlebury; the steel carpenter's square is invented by Silas Hawes of Shaftsbury

1816 — A famine year occurs, with frosts or snow in every month

1819 — Captain Alden Partridge establishes the first private military college in the nation, at Norwich; the college is later moved to Northfield

1823 — The Champlain-Hudson Canal opens, linking Vermont to New York City; the first Normal School, exclusively for the preparation of teachers, is established by Samuel Read Hall in Concord Corner

1834 — Thomas Davenport of Bradford invents the first electric motor

1844 — Horace Wells of White River Junction is the first person to use laughing gas as an anesthetic for pulling teeth

1848 — The first railroad and telegraph line in Vermont begins operation

1850 — The Vermont legislature nullifies the U.S. Fugitive Slave Law

1852 — The manufacture and sale of intoxicating liquor as a beverage is prohibited by law

1857 — The second state capitol is destroyed by fire and work on the new capitol begins

1862 — The first Land-Grant College Act, proposed by and named for Senator Justin Smith Morrill of Vermont, is signed by President Lincoln

1864 — In the northernmost action of the Civil War, Confederate soldiers raid St. Albans

1869 — The first agricultural society for dairymen, the Vermont Dairymen's Association, is organized in Montpelier; the first pulp paper mill is established by William A. Russell in Bellows Falls

1881 — Chester A. Arthur, born in Fairfield, becomes the twenty-first president of the United States

1896—Vermont becomes the first state to enact an absentee voting law

1910—The first long-distance hiking trail, Vermont's 262-mi. (422-km) Long Trail, is begun

1923—Calvin Coolidge, born in Plymouth Notch, becomes the thirtieth president of the United States and is sworn into office in Plymouth Notch

1927—Severe flooding of the Winooski River and branches of the Connecticut River kill sixty persons and cause millions of dollars in damage

1934—The first ski tow in the United States opens in Woodstock on Clinton Gilbert's farm

1935—The first state symphony orchestra in the country is organized, with Alan Carter of Rutland as the conductor

1938—A hurricane does more than $12 million in damage and causes five deaths

1940—Ida M. Fuller of Ludlow receives check No. 00-000-001 for $22.54, the first Social Security benefit payment; the first chair lift is used on Mount Mansfield

1941—The first wind turbine used to generate power for an alternating-current power system is operated at Grandpa's Knob in Castleton; the United States enters World War II

1946—Senator Warren R. Austin of Vermont is appointed the first U.S. delegate to the United Nations Security Council; *Vermont Life* begins publication

1947—Vermont's state police force is established; Helen E. Burbank, appointed secretary of state, is the first woman to serve as a state officer

1952—Andrea Mead Lawrence of Rutland is the first American to win two Olympic gold medals in skiing

1954—Consuelo N. Bailey becomes the first woman in the United States to be elected lieutenant governor; the first television station in the state begins broadcasting

1958—William H. Meyer, the first Democrat since 1854, is elected to Congress from Vermont

1959—Vermont and New York celebrate the 350th anniversary of the discovery of Lake Champlain

1962—Vermonters elect their first Democratic governor since 1853, Philip H. Hoff

1964—Lyndon B. Johnson is the first Democratic presidential candidate to receive Vermont's electoral votes since 1856

1965—Historic "one town/one vote" representation in the Vermont General Assembly ends with court-ordered reapportionment requiring "one person/one vote" representation; the Vermont house of representatives goes from 246 members to 150; the number of Vermont senators remains at 30

1970—The landmark Environmental Control Law, Act 250, is passed by the legislature; an Environmental Conservation Agency is established

1971—Amtrak selects a New England route through Vermont for its Washington, D.C.-to-Montreal passenger trains, reinstating passenger train service discontinued in 1966

1973—The worst flood since 1927 causes three deaths and an estimated $65 million in damage

1974—Senator George D. Aiken announces plans to retire after serving thirty-four years in the U.S. Congress; Vermont voters choose their first Democratic senator since the 1880s, Patrick J. Leahy, to succeed Aiken

1976—The first American medal, a silver, in an Olympic cross-country skiing event is won by Bill Koch of Guilford; Tad Coffin of Strafford wins the first American gold medal in the Olympic three-day individual equestrian event; Governor Thomas P. Salmon gives official status to Vermont's Abenaki Indians so that, among other things, they can qualify for certain federal benefits

1977—Governor Richard A. Snelling revokes Governor Salmon's recognition of the status of the Abenakis; Vermont celebrates the two-hundredth birthday of the founding of the independent state of Vermont

1980—A nearly snowless winter causes wells to run dry, water lines to freeze, and the ski industry to suffer

1982—Nearly 180 Vermont towns, at their annual town meetings, pass resolutions calling for a nuclear freeze

1985—Madeleine Kunin is elected the first woman governor of Vermont

1988—The Growth Management Act, Act 200, another landmark environmental law, is passed, calling for community plans to promote preservation of natural resources and historic landmarks and to control development

1990—Bernard Sanders is elected Vermont's U.S. representative, becoming the first Socialist to be elected to the U.S. House in sixty years

1991—Vermont celebrates its bicentennial

SHERMAN ADAMS

ETHAN ALLEN

CHESTER A. ARTHUR

SARAH CLEGHORN

IMPORTANT PEOPLE

Sherman Adams (1899-1986), born in East Dover; politician, government official; New Hampshire state legislator (1941-45); U.S. representative (1945-49); governor (1949-53); assistant to President Dwight D. Eisenhower (1953-58)

George David Aiken (1892-1984), born in Dummerston; politician, farmer; pioneered the commercial cultivation of wildflowers; Vermont state legislator (1931-35); lieutenant governor (1935-37); governor (1937-41); U.S. senator (1941-75)

Ethan Allen (1737-1789), patriot, soldier, author; settled in the New Hampshire Grants in 1769; formed and led the Green Mountain Boys (1770-75); captured Fort Ticonderoga (1775); was captured and held prisoner by the British (1775-78); farmed near Burlington (1780-89); wrote pamphlets and books about the conflicting claims to Vermont, about his captivity by the British, and against religion (*Reason, the Only Oracle of Man*)

Ira Allen (1751-1814), political leader, author; brother of Ethan Allen; served with the Green Mountain Boys; wrote the preamble to the constitution of independent Vermont (1777); led the fight for statehood; donated land to build the University of Vermont; authored *Natural and Political History of the State of Vermont* (1798)

Chester A. Arthur (1830-1886), born in Fairfield; twenty-first president of the United States (1881-85); U.S. vice-president (1881); became president after the assassination of President James A. Garfield

Warren Robinson Austin (1877-1962), born in Highgate; politician, diplomat; U.S. senator (1931-46); head of the first U.S. delegation to the United Nations (1946-53)

William Alwyn "Snowflake" Bentley (1865-1931), born in Jericho; meteorologist, photographer; discovered that no two snowflakes are alike by studying pictures of them taken with a camera that he had combined with a microscope lens

Samuel de Champlain (1567?-1635), French explorer, fur trader, political leader; discovered the lake named for him, Lake Champlain; claimed the region of Vermont for France

Thomas Chittenden (1730-1797), politician; helped write Vermont's constitution (1777); first governor of the independent state of Vermont (1778-89); first governor of the state of Vermont (1791-97)

Sarah Cleghorn (1876-1959), reformer, writer; raised in Manchester; worked for rights of children and animals, for the abolition of capital punishment, and for pacifism; wrote poetry, fiction, and articles about social concerns

Zerah Colburn (1804-1839), born in Cabot; teacher, clergyman; a mathematical genius who, before he could read or write, could multiply two six-digit numbers in his head, calculating the correct answer in seconds; Methodist minister; taught languages at Norwich University

Jacob Collamer (1791-1865), jurist, politician; Vermont state legislator (1821-22, 1827-28); Vermont supreme-court judge (1833-42); U.S. representative (1843-49); U.S. postmaster general (1849-50); U.S. senator (1855-65)

Calvin Coolidge (1872-1933), born in Plymouth Notch; thirtieth president of the United States (1923-29); lieutenant governor of Massachusetts (1916); governor of Massachusetts (1919-21); U.S. vice-president (1921-23); became president after the death of President Warren G. Harding

Thomas Davenport (1802-1851), born in Williamstown; inventor; fashioned the first electric motor on record (1834); invented a small electric train, an electric printing press, and an electric piano

John Deere (1804-1886), born in Rutland; inventor, industrialist; invented the first steel plow; manufactured plows and tractors at Deere and Company

George Dewey (1837-1917), born in Montpelier; naval officer; served under Admiral David Farragut in the Civil War; commanded the Asian squadron during the Spanish-American War and captured Manila (1898); admiral (1899-1917)

John Dewey (1859-1952), born in Burlington; philosopher, psychologist, educator, writer; developed the philosophy of pragmatism; led the progressive education movement; founded the American Association of University Professors (1915)

Stephen A. Douglas (1813-1861), born in Brandon; lawyer, politician; practiced law in Illinois; U.S. representative for Illinois (1843-47); U.S. senator for Illinois (1847-61); engaged in famous debates with Abraham Lincoln (1858)

George Franklin Edmunds (1828-1919), born in Richmond; lawyer, politician; Vermont state representative (1854-59); Vermont state senator (1861-62); U.S. senator (1866-91); helped draft the Civil Rights Act (1875) and the Sherman Antitrust Act (1890)

Erastus Fairbanks (1792-1864), manufacturer, politician; associated with his brother Thaddeus's business; governor (1852-53, 1860-61)

Thaddeus Fairbanks (1796-1886), inventor, manufacturer; invented and patented the first platform scale (1831); invented a draft mechanism for furnaces (1843); invented a hot water heater (1881); formed the E. & T. Fairbanks & Company with his brother Erastus to manufacture platform scales

JOHN DEERE

JOHN DEWEY

STEPHEN A. DOUGLAS

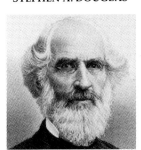

THADDEUS FAIRBANKS

DOROTHY CANFIELD FISHER

ROBERT FROST

RICHARD M. HUNT

CARRIE KILGORE

Dorothy Canfield Fisher (1879-1958), writer; spent most of her adult life in Arlington; wrote novels and nonfiction books for adults and children, including *The Squirrel Cage, Understood Betsy,* and *American Portraits*

Ralph Edward Flanders (1880-1970), born in Barnet; engineer, politician, editor, manufacturer; U.S. senator (1947-59); although a Republican, he supported the Truman Doctrine and the Marshall Plan and led the move to censure Senator Joseph McCarthy during the anticommunism hearings

Robert L. Frost (1874-1963), poet; maintained a home on a Vermont farm near South Shaftsbury from 1920; cofounded Middlebury College's Bread Loaf School and Writers' Conference (1920); won four Pulitzer Prizes in poetry (1924, 1931, 1937, 1943), one of which was for the collection of poems *New Hampshire* in which he boasted that New Hampshire was "one of the two best states in the Union"—Vermont, of course, was the other; owned a summer home called Shingled Cottage not far from Bread Loaf Mountain near Ripton; Poet Laureate of Vermont (1961)

James Hartness (1861-1934), inventor, engineer, politician; helped standardize screw threads; governor of Vermont (1921-23)

Abby Maria Hemenway (1828-1890), born in Ludlow; teacher, historian; compiled and edited *Vermont Historical Gazetteer,* a five-volume history of Vermont

Blanche Honneggar-Moyse (1909-   ), musician, director; cofounded the Marlboro School of Music (1951); founded the New England Bach Festival (1969) at Brattleboro and is the current artistic director

Richard Morris Hunt (1827-1895), born in Brattleboro; architect; brother of William Morris Hunt; designed the first office building with elevators and John Astor's country house, Biltmore, in Asheville, North Carolina; other designs included the main section of the Metropolitan Museum of Art in New York City and the National Observatory in Washington, D.C.

William Morris Hunt (1824-1879), born in Brattleboro; painter; brother of Richard Morris Hunt; painted *Girl Reading* and *Hurdy-Gurdy Boy;* his works hang in the Metropolitan Museum of Art

Carrie Burnham Kilgore (1838-1909), born in Craftsbury; teacher, lawyer, advocate of women's rights; became the first woman graduate of the University of Pennsylvania Law School (1883); the first woman master in chancery in Pennsylvania; admitted to plead cases before the United States Supreme Court (1890)

Madeleine Kunin (1933-   ), journalist, politician; reporter for the *Burlington Free Press;* Vermont state representative (1973-79); lieutenant governor (1979-83); governor (1985-91)

Sinclair Lewis (1885-1951), novelist; he called himself a Vermonter by adoption, lived in Barnard for a number of years with wife Dorothy Thompson; was the first American to win the Nobel Prize in literature (1930); wrote *Main Street, Babbitt,* and *Elmer Gantry,* all critical of various aspects of American life; one of his books, *It Can't Happen Here* (1935), was set in Vermont

Matthew Lyon (1750-1822), soldier, politician, entrepreneur; aided in the capture of Fort Ticonderoga; was an officer in the Green Mountain Boys; U.S. representative (1797-1801); built and operated paper mills and established a printing office

George Perkins Marsh (1801-1882), born in Woodstock; author, lawyer, diplomat; cousin of James Marsh; as a U.S. representative (1848-49), he supported high tariffs and opposed slavery and the Mexican War; U.S. minister to Turkey (1849-54); U.S. minister to Italy (1860-82); wrote *Man and Nature* (1864), revised as *The Earth as Modified by Human Action* (1874), which was described as "the fountainhead of the conservation movement"

James Marsh (1794-1842), born in Hartford; author, philosopher, educator; cousin of George Perkins Marsh; president, University of Vermont (1826-33); was a strong influence on the transcendentalist movement

Larkin Goldsmith Mead (1835-1910), sculptor; brother of William Rutherford Mead; designed the Lincoln Tomb in Springfield, Illinois; created statues of Ethan Allen for the Vermont capital and for the Capitol in Washington, D.C.

William Rutherford Mead (1846-1928), born in Brattleboro; architect; brother of Larkin Goldsmith Mead; designed the Rhode Island State House and the Boston Public Library; president of the American Academy in Rome (1909-27)

Samuel Morey (1762-1843), inventor; constructed a paddlewheel steamboat in Fairlee and sailed it up the Connecticut River (1793); Lake Morey is named after him; built the first internal-combustion engine equipped with a carburetor (1826)

Justin Smith Morrill (1810-1898), born in Strafford; politician; served forty-four consecutive years in Congress as a U.S. representative (1855-67) and a U.S. senator (1867-99); sponsored the Morrill Tariff Act (1861) and the Morrill Land-Grant College Act (1862)

Levi Parsons Morton (1824-1920), born in Shoreham; banker, politician; U.S. representative from New York (1879-91); U.S. minister to France (1881-85); vice-president of the United States (1889-93); governor of New York (1895-97)

Clarina Howard Nichols (1810-1885), born in West Townshend; reformer, editor; edited the *Windham County Democrat;* influenced the woman suffrage movement through her editorials and by lobbying to improve laws giving more rights to women

SINCLAIR LEWIS

JAMES MARSH

JUSTIN MORRILL

CLARINA NICHOLS

JOHN NOYES

HIRAM POWERS

JOSEPH SMITH

ALEKSANDR SOLZHENITSYN

John Humphrey Noyes (1811-1886), born in Brattleboro; minister, social reformer; formulated the doctrine of Perfectionism and formed a community based on common ownership of property; arrested for his views on free love (1846); fled to New York and founded the Oneida Community (1848)

Elisha Graves Otis (1811-1861), born near Halifax; inventor; invented safety devices for elevators; patented a steam elevator (1860); founded the Otis elevator company

Hiram Powers (1805-1873), born in Woodstock; sculptor; created statues of Franklin and Jefferson that are in the Capitol in Washington, D.C.

Redfield Proctor (1831-1908), born in Proctorsville; businessman, lawyer; founded the Vermont Marble Company; governor (1878-80); U.S. secretary of war (1889-91); U.S. senator (1891-1908)

Bernard Sanders (1941-   ), politician; Socialist mayor of Burlington (1981-89); U.S. representative (1991-   )

Frank Pierce Sargent (1854-1908), born in East Orange; labor leader; headed the Brotherhood of Locomotive Firemen (1885-1902)

James Sargent (1824-1910), born in Chester; inventor; devised and manufactured the "nonpickable" combination lock and the time lock; invented railway semaphore signals, automatic fire alarms, and glass-lined steel tanks

Rudolph Serkin (1903-   ), pianist, composer; helped found and acted as president and artistic director of the Marlboro Festival and School of Music

Joseph Smith (1805-1844), born in Sharon; Mormon prophet; published the *Book of Mormon*; founded the Church of Jesus Christ of Latter-day Saints

Robert Holbrook Smith (1879-1950), born in St. Johnsbury; surgeon; cofounded Alcoholics Anonymous with fellow former-Vermonter William G. Wilson (1935) in New York

Aleksandr Isayevich Solzhenitsyn (1918-   ), novelist and historian; won the 1970 Nobel Prize for literature; exiled from the U.S.S.R. (1974) for actions allegedly incompatible with Soviet citizenship; moved to United States (1976) and settled on a farm near Cavendish; wrote *Cancer Ward* (1968), *August 1914* (1971), *The Gulag Archipelago* (1973), *A World Split Apart* (1979)

Alphonso Taft (1810-1891), born in Townshend; jurist, politician; U.S. secretary of war (1876); U.S. attorney general (1876-77); U.S. minister to Austria-Hungary (1882-84)

Daniel Pierce Thompson (1795-1868), author, judge; probate judge (1837-40, 1841-42); a clerk of the county court (1844-46); Vermont secretary of state (1853-55); described Vermont's history in novels, including *The Green Mountain Boys*

Dorothy Thompson (1894-1961), journalist, author; wrote from Vienna (1920-24) and Berlin (1924-28); syndicated columnist (1936-57); wrote *New Russia* (1928) and *The Courage to Be Happy* (1957); called Barnard home from the 1930s until she died; buried in Barnard Cemetery

DOROTHY THOMPSON

Maria von Trapp (1905-1987), musician, lecturer, author; married Baron Georg von Trapp (1927) and became the second mother to his seven children; escaped with the family from Hitler's Austria (1938) and finally settled in Stowe (1942); her award-winning *Story of the Trapp Family Singers* was made into a stage musical and the movie *Sound of Music*

Royall Tyler (1757-1826), playwright, jurist; wrote the first comedy by an American, *The Contrast*, produced by a professional company in New York City (1787); wrote many other plays, verse, and prose; state's attorney for Windham County (1794-1801); assistant state supreme court judge (1801-07); chief justice (1807-13)

WILLIAM WILSON

Seth Warner (1743-1784), soldier; helped form and lead the Green Mountain Boys; led the forces that seized Crown Point (1775) and won the Battle of Bennington (August 16, 1777)

Electra Havemeyer Webb (1888-1960), museum founder; owned a summer home near Shelburne; founded the Shelburne Museum (1947), the largest and most famous of Vermont's seventy-four museums

Horace Wells (1815-1848), born in Hartford; dentist, anesthetist; was the first to use laughing gas (nitrous oxide combined with oxygen) as an anesthetic before extracting a tooth (1844)

THOMAS W. WOOD

Emma Hart Willard (1787-1870), educator; pioneered higher education for women; established a girls' boarding school at Middlebury (1814) where she proved that girls could master such subjects as mathematics and philosophy without losing their health, refinement, or charm

William G. Wilson (1895-1971), born in East Dorset; securities analyst; cofounded Alcoholics Anonymous with fellow former-Vermonter Robert Holbrook Smith (1935) in New York

Thomas Waterman Wood (1823-1903), born in Montpelier; painter; depicted blacks during the Civil War; painted portraits of important New Yorkers; established the Wood Gallery of Art in Montpelier

BRIGHAM YOUNG

Brigham Young (1801-1877), born in Whitingham; religious leader; second president of the Mormon Church (1847); organized and directed the settlement of Mormons in Salt Lake City; first governor of the Utah Territory (1849-57)

GOVERNORS

Thomas Chittenden	1791-1797		Carroll S. Page	1890-1892
Paul Brigham	1797		Levi K. Fuller	1892-1894
Isaac Tichenor	1797-1807		Urban A. Woodbury	1894-1896
Israel Smith	1807-1808		Josiah Grout	1896-1898
Isaac Tichenor	1808-1809		Edward C. Smith	1898-1900
Jonas Galusha	1809-1813		William W. Stickney	1900-1902
Martin Chittenden	1813-1815		John G. McCullough	1902-1904
Jonas Galusha	1815-1820		Charles J. Bell	1904-1906
Richard Skinner	1820-1823		Fletcher D. Proctor	1906-1908
Cornelius P. Van Ness	1823-1826		George H. Prouty	1908-1910
Ezra Butler	1826-1828		John A. Mead	1910-1912
Samuel C. Crafts	1828-1831		Allen M. Fletcher	1912-1915
William A. Palmer	1831-1835		Charles W. Gates	1915-1917
Silas H. Jenison	1835-1841		Horace F. Graham	1917-1919
Charles Paine	1841-1843		Percival W. Clement	1919-1921
John Mattocks	1843-1844		James Hartness	1921-1923
William Slade	1844-1846		Redfield Proctor	1923-1925
Horace Eaton	1846-1848		Franklin S. Billings	1925-1927
Carlos Coolidge	1848-1850		John E. Weeks	1927-1931
Charles K. Williams	1850-1852		Stanley C. Wilson	1931-1935
Erastus Fairbanks	1852-1853		Charles M. Smith	1935-1937
John S. Robinson	1853-1854		George D. Aiken	1937-1941
Stephen Royce	1854-1856		William H. Wills	1941-1945
Ryland Fletcher	1856-1858		Mortimer R. Proctor	1945-1947
Hiland Hall	1858-1860		Ernest W. Gibson	1947-1950
Erastus Fairbanks	1860-1861		Harold J. Arthur	1950-1951
Frederick Holbrook	1861-1863		Lee E. Emerson	1951-1955
John Gregory Smith	1863-1865		Joseph B. Johnson	1955-1959
Paul Dillingham	1865-1867		Robert T. Stafford	1959-1961
John B. Page	1867-1869		F. Ray Keyser, Jr.	1961-1963
Peter T. Washburn	1869-1870		Philip H. Hoff	1963-1969
George W. Hendee	1870		Deane C. Davis	1969-1973
John W. Stewart	1870-1872		Thomas P. Salmon	1973-1977
Julius Converse	1872-1874		Richard A. Snelling	1977-1985
Asahel Peck	1874-1876		Madeleine M. Kunin	1985-1991
Horace Fairbanks	1876-1878		Richard A. Snelling	1991-
Redfield Proctor	1878-1880			
Roswell Farnham	1880-1882			
John L. Barstow	1882-1884			
Samuel E. Pingree	1884-1886			
Ebenezer J. Ormsbee	1886-1888			
William P. Dillingham	1888-1890			

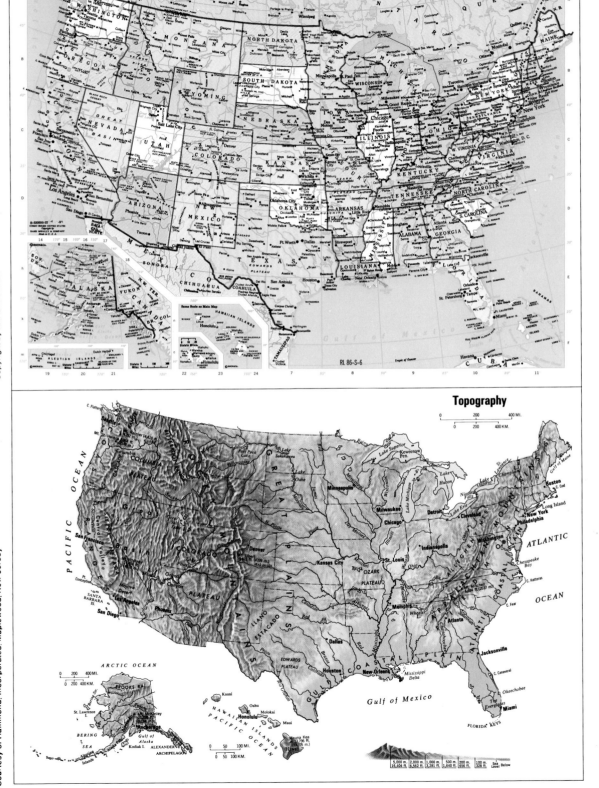

Topography

MAP KEY

Adams Mountain (mountain) C3
Albany B4
Alburg B2
Alder Brook (brook) B4
Andover E3
Arlington E2
Arrowhead Mountain Lake (reservoir) B2
Ascutney E4
Bakersfield B3
Bald Mountain (mountain) B5
Ball Mountain Lake (reservoir) E3
Baltimore E3
Barnard D3
Barnet C4
Barre C4
Barton B4
Barton River (river) B4
Bartonsville E3
Baten Kill River (river) E2
Beebe Plain A4
Beecher Falls A5
Bellows Falls E4
Belmont E3
Belvidere Mountain (mountain) B3
Bennington F2
Berkshire B3
Berlin C3
Berlin Corners C3
Bethel D3
Black Creek (creek) B3
Black River (river) E3
Black River (river) B4
Bloomfield B5
Bluff Mountain (mountain) B5
Bomoseen D2
Bomoseen Lake (lake) D2
Bradford D4
Brandon D2
Brattleboro F3
Bread Loaf Mountain (mountain) C3
Bridgewater D3
Bridgewater Corners D3
Bridport D2
Brighton B5
Bristol C2
Bromley Mountain (mountain) E3
Brookfield C3
Brookline E3
Browns River (river) B2
Brunswick B5
Burke B5
Burlington C2
Cabot C4
Cadys Falls B3
Calais C4
Cambridge B3
Cambridgeport E3
Camels Hump Mountain (mountain) C3
Canaan A5
Castleton D2
Cavendish E3
Center Rutland D2
Charlotte C2
Chelsea D4
Chester E3
Chester Depot E3
Chittenden D3
Chittenden Reservoir (reservoir) D3
Clarendon D3
Clarendon River (river) E2
Clarendon Springs D2
Colchester B2
Cold Hollow Mountains (mountains) B3
Colton Hill (hill) D4
Concord C5
Connecticut River (river) E4
Coventry B4
Craftsbury B4
Craftsbury Common B4
Crystal Lake (lake) B4
Cuttingsville E3
Danby E3
Danville C4
Dead Creek (creek) C2
Deerfield River (river) F3
Derby B4
Derby Line A4
Dog River (river) C3
Dorset E2
Dorset Peak (peak) E2
Duxbury C3
East Arlington E2
East Barre C4

East Berkshire B3
East Bethel D3
East Burke B5
East Calais C4
East Concord C5
East Dorset E2
East Dover F3
East Dummerston F3
East Fairfield B3
East Hardwick B4
East Highgate B3
East Middlebury D2
East Montpelier C4
East Poultney D2
East Randolph D3
East Ryegate C4
East St. Johnsbury C5
East Wallingford E3
Echo Lake (lake) B5
Ellen Mountain (mountain) C3
Elmore B3
Enosburg B3
Enosburg Falls B3
Essex B2
Essex Junction C2
Fair Haven D2
Fairfax B2
Fairfield B3
Fairfield Pond (pond) B2
Fairlee D4
Fayston C3
Ferrisburg C2
Forest Dale D2
Foxville C4
Franklin B3
Furnace Brook (brook) D3
Gaysville D3
Georgia B2
Georgia Center B2
Gihon River (river) B3
Gilman C5
Glastenbury Mountain (mountain) F2
Glover B4
Gore Mountain (mountain) B5
Grafton E3
Grand Isle B2
Graniteville C4
Granville D3
Grassy Brook (brook) E3
Great Averill Pond (pond) B5
Green Mountains (mountains) F2
Green River (river) F3
Green River Reservoir (reservoir) B3
Groton C4
Guilford F3
Hancock D3
Hardwick B4
Harriman Reservoir (reservoir) F3
Hartford D4
Hartland D4
Hartland Four Corners D4
Herrick Mountain (mountain) D2
Highgate Center B2
Highgate Falls B2
Hinesburg C2
Hubbardton River (river) D2
Huntington C3
Hyde Park B3
Hydeville D2
Irasburg B4
Island Pond B5
Island Pond (pond) B5
Jacksonville F3
Jamaica E3
Jay Peak (peak) B3
Jeffersonville B3
Jericho B3
Joes Brook (brook) C4
Johnson B3
Jonesville C3
Killington Peak (peak) D3
Kirby C5
La Motte Isle (island) B2
La Platte River (river) C2
Lake Carmi (lake) B3
Lake Caspian (lake) B4
Lake Champlain (lake) B2
Lake Dunmore (lake) D2
Lake Hortonia (lake) D2
Lake Iroquois (lake) C2
Lake Memphremagog (lake) B4

Lake Morey (lake) D4
Lake Salem (lake) B4
Lake Willoughby (lake) B4
Lamoille River (river) B3
Lamoille River North Branch B3
Lemon Fair River (river) D2
Lewis Creek (creek) C2
Lincoln C3
Little Otter Creek (creek) C2
Little Waterbury River (river) C3
Londonderry E3
Lowell B4
Lowell Mountains (mountains) B4
Lower Village C3
Ludlow E3
Ludlow Mountain (mountain) E3
Lunenburg C5
Lyndon B4
Lyndon Center B4
Lyndonville B4
Mad River (river) C3
Maidstone B5
Maidstone Lake (lake) B5
Malletts Bay (bay) B2
Manchester E2
Manchester Center E2
Marlboro F3
Marshfield C4
McIndoe Falls C4
Mettawee River (river) E2
Middlebury C2
Middlesex C2
Middletown Springs E2
Miles Mountain (mountain) C5
Mill Brook (brook) B5
Miller Run (river) B4
Milton B2
Missisquoi Bay (bay) A2
Missisquoi River (river) B3
Monadnock Mountain (mountain) B5
Monkton C2
Montgomery B3
Montgomery Center B3
Montpelier C3
Moore Reservoir (reservoir) C5
Moose River (river) B5
Moretown C3
Morrisville B3
Moscow C3
Mount Ascutney (mountain) E4
Mount Holly E3
Mount Mansfield (mountain) B3
Mount Pisgah (mountain) F3
New Haven River (river) C2
Newbury C4
Newport B4
Newport Center B4
North Bennington F2
North Clarendon D3
North Concord C5
North Hartland D4
North Hartland Reservoir (reservoir) D4
North Hero B2
North Hero Island (island) B2
North Hyde Park B3
North Montpelier C4
North Pownal F2
North Springfield E4
North Springfield Reservoir (reservoir) E4
North Troy A4
North Westminster E4
Northfield C3
Northfield Center C3
Northfield Falls C3
Northfield Mountains (mountains) C3
Norton Pond (pond) B5
Norwich D4
Nulhegan River (river) B5
Old Bennington F2
Olga Mountain (mountain) F3
Ompompanoosuc River (river) D4
Ompompanoosuc River, West Branch D4
Orleans B4
Orwell D2
Ottauquechee River (river) D3
Otter Creek (creek) C2
Paper Mill Village F2
Passumpsic C4
Passumpsic River (river) C4
Paul Stream (stream) B5
Pawlet E2
Peacham C4
Peacham Pond (pond) C4
Perkinsville E3
Peru E3
Pittsford D2
Plainfield C4
Plymouth Union D3
Post Mills D4
Poultney D2
Poultney River (river) D2
Pownal F2
Pownal Center F2
Proctor E3
Putney F3
Quechee D4
Randolph D3
Randolph Center D3
Reading E3
Readsboro F3
Richford B3
Richmond C3
Ripton D2
Riverton C3
Rochester D3
Rochester Mountain (mountain) D3
Roxbury C3
Rutland D3
St. Albans B2
St. Albans Bay B2
St. Albans Bay (bay) B2
St. Catherine Lake (lake) E2

St. George C2
St. Johnsbury C4
St. Johnsbury Center C4
Salisbury D2
Saxtons River E3
Saxtons River (river) E3
Seymour Lake (lake) B4
Shaftsbury E2
Sharon D4
Sheffield B4
Shelburne C2
Shelburne Pond (pond) C2
Sheldon B3
Sheldon Springs B3
Sherburne D3
Signal Mountain (mountain) C4
Snake Mountain (mountain) C2
Somerset Reservoir (reservoir) E3
South Barre C3
South Burlington C2
South Dorset E2
South Hero B2
South Hero Island (island) B2
South Londonderry E3
South Royalton D3
South Rygate C4
South Wallingford E3
Springfield E4
Stamford F2
Stone Mountain (mountain) B5
Stowe C3
Stratton E3
Stratton Mountain (mountain) E3
Sunderland E2
Sunset Lake (lake) D2
Swanton B2
Taftsville D4
The Dome (mountain) F2
Thetford D4
Thetford Center D4
Topsham C4
Townshend E3
Townshend Reservoir (reservoir) E3
Troy B4
Trout River (river) B3
Tyler Branch (branch) B3
Underhill B3
Underhill Center B3
Union Village Reservoir (reservoir) D4
Upper Graniteville C4
Vergennes C2
Vernon F2
Victory C5
Waits River (river) C4
Waitsfield C3
Wallingford E3
Walloomsac River (river) F2
Waltham C2
Wardsboro E3
Warren C3
Washington C4
Waterbury C3
Waterbury Center C3
Waterbury Reservoir (reservoir) C3
Waterford B4
Weathersfield E4
Websterville C4
Wells E2
Wells River C4
Wells River (river) C4
West Burke B5
West Charleston B4
West Danville C4
West Dover F3
West Dummerston F3
West Fairlee D4
West Halifax F3
West Hartford D4
West Lincoln C2
West Mountain (mountain) B5
West Newbury C4
West Pawlet E2
West River (river) E3
West Rupert E2
West Rutland D2
West Topsham C4
West Townshend E3
West Wardsboro E3
West Windsor E4
West Woodstock D3
Westfield B4
Westford B2
Westminster E4
Weston E3
Wheelock B4
Wheelock Mountain (mountain) B4
White Face Mountain (mountain) B3
White River (river) D4
White River Junction D4
Whiting D2
Whitingham F3
Wild Branch (branch) B4
Wilder D4
Willard Stream (stream) B5
Williams River (river) E3
Williamstown C3
Williamsville F3
Williston C2
Wilmington F3
Windsor E4
Winhall E3
Winona Lake (lake) C2
Winooski C2
Winooski River (river) C3
Winooski River, North Branch C3
Wolcott B4
Woodbury Mountain (mountain) C4
Woodstock D3
Worcester C3
Worcester Mountains (mountains) C3
Wrightsville Reservoir (reservoir) C3

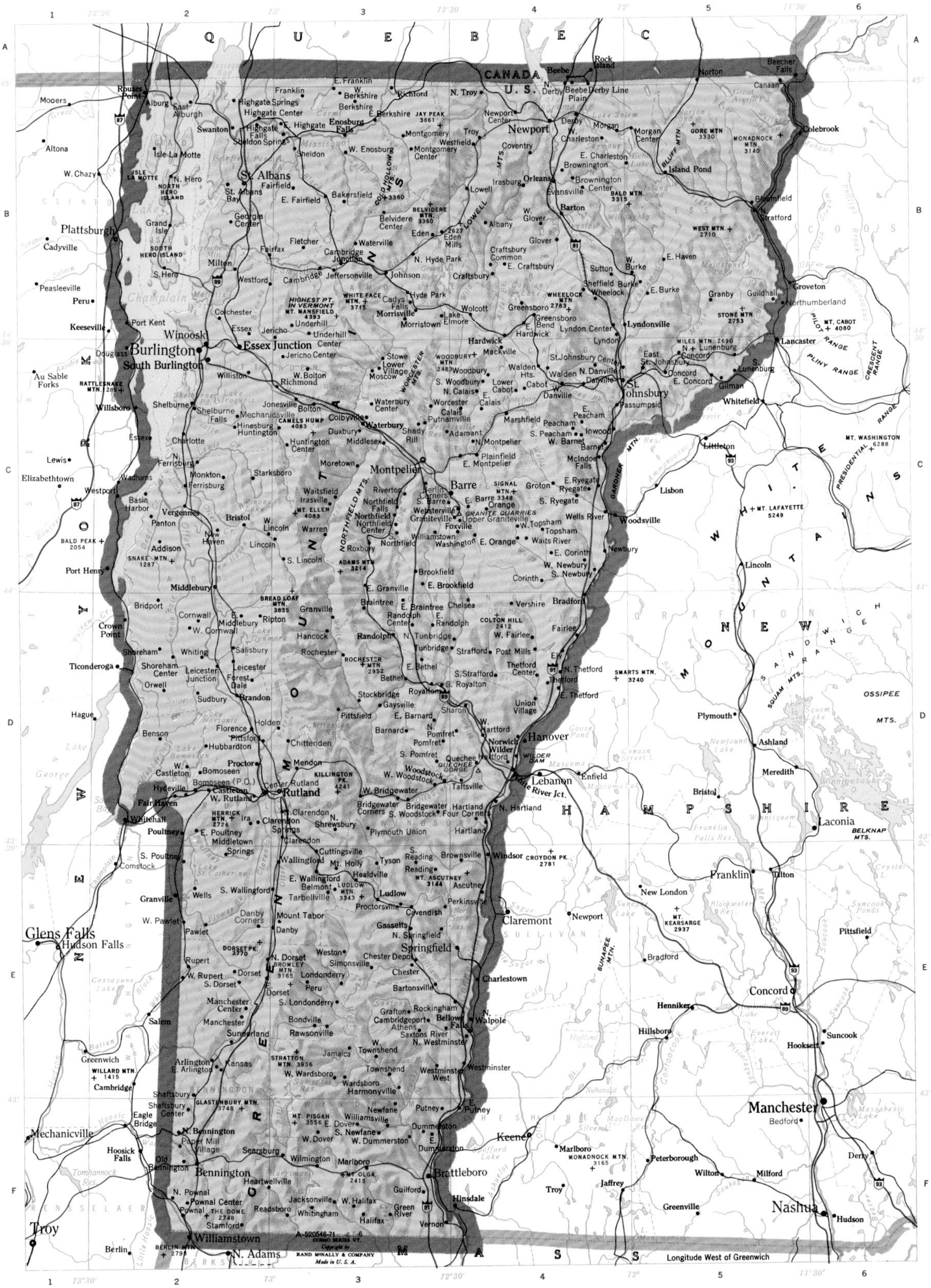

QUEBEC

CANADA
U.S.

NEW HAMPSHIRE

MASS.

Longitude West of Greenwich

Burlington
South Burlington
Essex Junction
Winooski
St. Albans
Montpelier
Barre
Rutland
Newport
Johnsbury
Hanover
Lebanon
Brattleboro
Bennington

Plattsburgh
Glens Falls
Troy
Manchester
Nashua
Concord
Claremont
Springfield
Keene

HIGHEST PT. IN VERMONT
MT. MANSFIELD 4393

CAMELS HUMP 4083

MT. ELLEN 4083

GREEN MOUNTAINS

WHITE MOUNTAINS

PRESIDENTIAL RANGE

MT. WASHINGTON 6288

MT. LAFAYETTE 5249

Lake Champlain

Lake Memphremagog

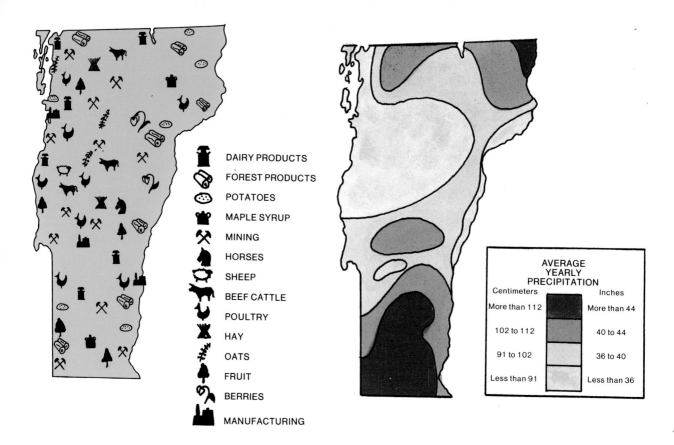

DAIRY PRODUCTS

FOREST PRODUCTS

POTATOES

MAPLE SYRUP

MINING

HORSES

SHEEP

BEEF CATTLE

POULTRY

HAY

OATS

FRUIT

BERRIES

MANUFACTURING

AVERAGE
YEARLY
PRECIPITATION

Centimeters		Inches
More than 112		More than 44
102 to 112		40 to 44
91 to 102		36 to 40
Less than 91		Less than 36

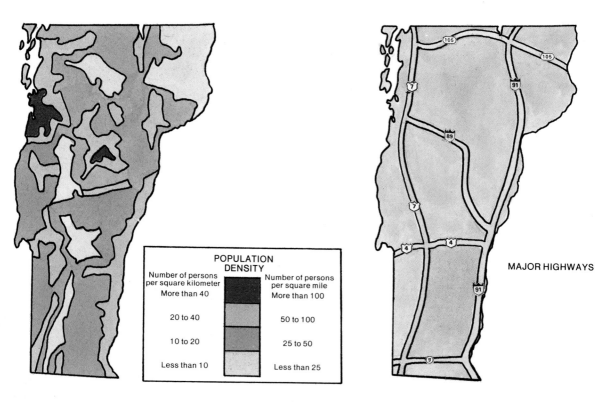

POPULATION
DENSITY

Number of persons per square kilometer		Number of persons per square mile
More than 40		More than 100
20 to 40		50 to 100
10 to 20		25 to 50
Less than 10		Less than 25

MAJOR HIGHWAYS

TOPOGRAPHY

5,000 m.	2,000 m.	1,000 m.	500 m.	200 m.	100 m.	Sea	Below
16,404 ft.	6,562 ft.	3,281 ft.	1,640 ft.	656 ft.	328 ft.	Level	

Courtesy of Hammond, Incorporated
Maplewood, New Jersey

COUNTIES

Cow crossing, Tunbridge

INDEX

Page numbers that appear in boldface type indicate illustrations

A barn in North Pomfret

Picture Identifications

Front cover: The town of Waits River
Back cover: Hutchins covered bridge, near Montgomery Center
Pages 2-3: Sheep grazing near Peacham
Page 6: *Pensive Pals*, a Norman Rockwell illustration from the *Grandpa and Me* series
Pages 8-9: A Reading farm in early morning light
Page 18: A montage of Vermonters
Pages 24-25: Colonel John Stark at the Battle of Bennington
Pages 36-37: A water-powered mill on the Connecticut River near Guildhall
Page 54: President Calvin Coolidge (left) and Vice President Charles Gates Dawes on inauguration day, March 4, 1925
Page 66: The Vermont State House
Pages 80-81: *Crossing the Ferry*, an 1878 painting by Thomas Waterman Wood
Pages 92-93: Harvey's Mountain, in Caledonia County near Barnet
Page 108: Montage showing the state flag, state tree (sugar maple), state animal (Morgan horse), state butterfly (monarch butterfly), and state flower (red clover)

About the Author

Sylvia McNair writes books and articles about interesting places for adults and young people. She has traveled on all the continents and in every state. Vermont, however, is her favorite place because it was her childhood home. She attended grade school in South Royalton and graduated from Richford High School. "Writing this book has been a real pleasure for me," she says. "Each of the fifty states has its own beautiful spots and fascinating history, but Vermont's are especially close to my heart." McNair is an alumna of Oberlin College and lives in Evanston, Illinois.

Picture Acknowledgments

Front cover: © Vernon Sigl/**SuperStock;** 2-3: © **Richard W. Brown;** 4: © Michael Philip Manheim/**Marilyn Gartman Agency;** 5: © **Ted Levin;** 6: **Art from the Archives of Brown & Bigelow, Inc.;** 8-9: © Tom Algire Photography/**Tom Stack & Associates;** 11: © G. Hampfler/**H. Armstrong Roberts;** 13 (left): © W. H. Clark/**H. Armstrong Roberts;** 13 (right): © **James P. Rowan;** 14: © Lani Howe/**Photri;** 16 (left): © **Ted Levin;** 16 (right): © **Lynn M. Stone;** 17: © **Richard W. Brown;** 18 (top left): © Michael Philip Manheim/**Marilyn Gartman Agency;** 18 (top right and bottom left): © **Richard W. Brown;** 18 (bottom right): © **Joseph A. DiChello, Jr.;** 21 (left): © **Richard W. Brown;** 21 (right): © **Joseph A. DiChello, Jr.;** 24-25: **The Bettmann Archive;** 27: **North Wind Picture Archives;** 30: **The Bettmann Archive;** 35: © Bill Howe/**Photri;** 36-37: © Camerique/**H. Armstrong Roberts;** 39; © **Porterfield/Chickering;** 40: **Shelburne Museum, Shelburne, Vermont;** 41: **Sheldon Museum;** 43: **Historical Pictures Service, Chicago;** 44: **North Wind Picture Archives;** 45: **Sheldon Museum;** 47: **Peacham Historical Association, Peacham, Vermont;** 49 (left): **Sheldon Museum;** 49 (right): **Library of Congress;** 50: **Special Collections, University of Vermont Library;** 52: **Shelburne Museum, Shelburne, Vermont;** 53: **Sheldon Museum;** 54: **Courtesy Vermont Historical Society;** 56: **The Bettmann Archive;** 58 (left): **UPI/Bettmann;** 58 (right): © Ken Dequaine Photography/**Third Coast Stock Source;** 60: **AP/Wide World Photos;** 66: © M. Schneiders/**H. Armstrong Roberts;** 70 (left): © Doris DeWitt/**TSW-Click/Chicago Ltd.;** 70 (right): © **Porterfield/ Chickering;** 72 (left): © **Virginia R. Grimes;** 72 (right): © **Porterfield/Chickering;** 73 (left): © **Porterfield/Chickering;** 73 (right): © **Jeff Greenberg;** 75: © James Blank/**Root Resources;** 76 (left): © Lani Howe/**Photri;** 76 (right): © **Richard W. Brown;** 78 (top left and bottom left): © Ken Dequaine Photography/**Third Coast Stock Source;** 78 (top right): © H. Abernathy/**H. Armstrong Roberts;** 78 (bottom right): © **Photri;** 80-81: **In the collection of the T. W. Wood Art Gallery, Montpelier, Vermont;** 83 (left): © Lani Howe/**Photri;** 83 (right): **AP/Wide World Photos;** 84: © David Forbert/**SuperStock;** 87: © **1948 The Curtis Publishing Company;** 88 (both pictures): © **Jerry Hennen;** 91: © Lani Howe/**Photri;** 92-93: © **Richard W. Brown;** 95 (left): © F. Sieb/**H. Armstrong Roberts;** 95 (right): © H. Abernathy/**H. Armstrong Roberts;** 95 (map): **Len Meents;** 98 (left): © Eric Carle/**SuperStock;** 98 (right): © Damm/Zefa/**H. Armstrong Roberts;** 100 (left): © Michael Philip Manheim/**Marilyn Gartman Agency;** 100 (right): © **Porterfield/Chickering;** 101 (left): © **Photri;** 101 (map): **Len Meents;** 103 (left): © **Joseph A. DiChello, Jr.;** 103 (map): **Len Meents;** 104 (left): © Lani Howe/**Photri;** 104 (right): © Don & Pat Valenti/**TSW-Click/Chicago Ltd.;** 107 (left): © **Ted Levin;** 107 (map): **Len Meents;** 108 (background): © Ruth A. Smith/**Root Resources;** 108 (flag): **Courtesy Flag Research Center, Winchester, Massachusetts 01890;** 108 (horse): **Photo by Debra James, Courtesy of UVM Morgan Horse Farm;** 108 (butterfly and clover): © John Gerlach/**Tom Stack & Associates;** 112: © W. H. Clark/**H. Armstrong Roberts;** 114: © Lani Howe/**Photri;** 117: © **Porterfield/ Chickering;** 119: © Jim Scourletis/**North Wind Picture Archives;** 126 (Adams): **AP/Wide World Photos;** 126 (Allen): **The Bettmann Archive;** 126 (Arthur): **U.S. Bureau of Printing and Engraving;** 126 (Cleghorn): **Special Collections, University of Vermont Library;** 127 (Deere and Fairbanks): **Historical Pictures Service, Chicago;** 127 (Dewey): **AP/Wide World Photos;** 127 (Douglas): **Library of Congress;** 128 (Fisher): **Courtesy Vermont Historical Society;** 128 (Frost): **AP/Wide World Photos;** 128 (Hunt and Kilgore): **North Wind Picture Archives;** 129, (Lewis): **The Bettmann Archive;** 129 (Marsh): **North Wind Picture Archives;** 129 (Morrill): **Historical Pictures Service, Chicago;** 129 (Nichols): **Special Collections, University of Vermont Library;** 130 (Noyes, Powers, and Smith): **Historical Pictures Service, Chicago;** 130 (Solzhenitsyn): **AP/Wide World Photos;** 131 (Thompson, Wilson, and Young): **AP/Wide World Photos;** 131 (Wood): **North Wind Picture Archives;** 138: © **Richard W. Brown;** 141: © James Blank/**Root Resources;** back cover: © Ralph Krubner/**SuperStock**